Foul Deeds & Suspicious Deaths in and around Frome

Foul Deeds & Suspicious Deaths in and around

FROME

By

Mick Davis & David Lassman

PEN & SWORD
TRUE CRIME

First published in Great Britain in 2018 by
Pen & Sword True Crime
An imprint of
Pen & Sword Books Ltd
47 Church Street
Barnsley
South Yorkshire
S70 2AS

ISBN 978 1 52670 604 1

A CIP catalogue record for this book is available from the British Library.

Typeset in Plantin and ITC Benguiat by
SRJ Info Jnana System Pvt Ltd.

Printed and bound in England by CPI Group (UK) Ltd, Croydon, CR0 4YY.

Pen & Sword Books Limited incorporates the imprints of Atlas, Archaeology, Aviation, Discovery, Family History, Fiction, History, Maritime, Military, Military Classics, Politics, Select, Transport, True Crime, Air World, Frontline Publishing, Leo Cooper, Remember When, Seaforth Publishing, The Praetorian Press, Wharncliffe Local History, Wharncliffe Transport, Wharncliffe True Crime and White Owl.

For a complete list of Pen & Sword titles please contact
PEN & SWORD BOOKS LIMITED
47 Church Street, Barnsley, South Yorkshire, S70 2AS, England
E-mail: enquiries@pen-and-sword.co.uk
Website: www.pen-and-sword.co.uk

Contents

who seemingly had no reason to steal, rob or even murder, other than for the 'thrill' of it.

Regarding the decision as to what to leave out, there may seem to anyone with 'local' knowledge one or two glaring and obvious omissions, but there are good reasons for these. The murder in 1860 at Rode, lying five miles northeast from Frome, when Constance Kent brutally killed her younger step-brother is probably the most 'high-profile' absentee, but it was felt this case had been so thoroughly chronicled, most recently in Kate Summerscale's hugely popular *Suspicions of Mr Whicher*, that any short article would have added nothing more to the subject and displaced a lesser-known, but equally fascinating, case.

Another murder that gripped the country and generated national headlines at the time but does not feature in this current anthology, is that of 14-year-old Sarah Watts at West Woodlands, in September 1851. In this case though, it was one of the first to be considered and was indeed going to be included. However, the more research that was undertaken, the more it became obvious that the case warranted a whole volume of its own. The result was *The Awful Killing of Sarah Watts: A Story of Confessions, Acquittals and Jailbreaks*, written by the authors and also published by Pen & Sword in 2018.

Other, perhaps lesser-known, stories also omitted include the mysterious death of Maud Davies, the assassination of Thomas Thynne of Longleat, the kidnapping of Annette Twynyho from the Old Nunnery in Lower Keyford, the Beckington Witches, the Gentle Street murders, the weavers riot of 1713, and the financial catastrophes and misadventures of the Champneys family. These will hopefully all be included in future volumes, but for now, we hope you enjoy those fourteen tales of the felonious, the burglarious and the murderous, both foul and suspicious, which reside in the current anthology.

David Lassman & Mick Davis
August 2017

The authors have made every attempt to locate copyright holders of photographs not in their collection.

Chapter 1

Witchfinder Extraordinaire

Joseph Glanvill and the Saducismus Triumphatus, *1681*

On the surface there may seem little, if anything, to connect the infamous series of seventeenth-century witch trials in Salem, Massachusetts with Frome, but one of the most influential books written on witchcraft and a major source for the justification of the trials, was written by a former resident of the town.

Joseph Glanvill was born in 1636 in Plymouth and raised within a strict Puritan household; the Puritans were a group of English Reformed Protestants who sought to 'purify' the Church of England from its Catholic practices. He studied religion, logic and philosophy at Exeter College, Oxford, and graduated with a BA in 1655; three years later he obtained an MA from Lincoln College. During his university years, he was already achieving a reputation as a forward thinker and it wasn't long before these thoughts found their way into print.

One of the first books to bear Glanvill's name was published in 1661, when he was 25. It was called *The Vanity of Dogmatizing* and its main thesis was an attack on scholasticism and religious persecution. The author made a plea for religious toleration, along with upholding scientific method and freedom of thought. These would mark Glanvill's belief system for the rest of his life and the book itself gained him a Fellowship of the Royal Society.

Glanvill was, by all accounts, an intelligent man, whose zeal for science was matched only by a need to investigate the paranormal and warn others of its existence. His professional career though, took place within religious orders and his first appointment would be in Frome.

During the English Civil War, which had begun when Glanvill was 6 years old, the Puritans had tightened their grip on St John the Baptist's Church, in Frome. The church stood on the site of what was claimed to have been the Saxon one founded by St Aldhelm, circa AD 685, and which brought the town into existence. The Puritans, in accordance with Parliament's directive, replaced the Book of Common Prayer with the new Directory of Public Worship, while the symbols of royal power were destroyed, or as in many churches, covered over by white liming, once victory was secured by Oliver Cromwell and the Parliamentarians. Glanvill was 16 years old when Cromwell became Lord Protector.

When the monarchy was restored and Charles II became king, a reversion to the old religious ways was demanded. This manifested itself in law, through what became known as the Clarendon Code; a series of four statutes passed between 1661 and 1665. The first of these was The Corporation Act (1661), which required all municipal officials to take Anglican Communion. In Frome, John Humpfry, the vicar of St John's, went along with this change initially, but when the Act of Uniformity was passed the following year – restoring the Book of Common Prayer and making its use compulsory in religious services – Humpfry refused to comply and he, along with more than 2,000 other clergymen nationwide, lost his living.

The Uniformity Act (1662), more than any other, was responsible for the spread of non-conformity, and initially Humpfry, having been forced out of his living at St John's church, literally moved up the road to the Rook Lane Congregation. But when the fourth and final statute – The Five Mile Act (1665) – made it illegal for non-conformist clergyman to live within five miles of their former living, he was forced out of Frome completely.

John Humpfry's successor as vicar of Frome was Joseph Glanvill, who had become Chaplain to Sir James Thynne, of nearby Longleat, in May 1662, and took up his appointment as vicar in October the same year. While in this position, Glanvill further researched and developed his beliefs in the paranormal and gathered together various episodes and incidents that would inform, or be included within, his greatest work – *Saducismus Triumphatus*. Glanvill was one of the many Puritans who believed in the supernatural and used the bible as 'evidence' to prove the existence of ghosts, demons and witches. Taking it one step further, many men like Glanvill used the line in Exodus 22:18, 'Thou shalt not suffer a witch to live', as a divine justification to persecute any person accused of practising the dark arts.

The full title of Glanvill's 'masterpiece' was *Saducismus Triumphatus:* or *Full and Plain Evidence concerning Witches and apparitions.* The first part (translated literally) means Triumph over the Sadducees, with 'Sadducees' being the term Glanvill used for the scientists he knew who were sceptical of the existence of the paranormal or those who tried to explain away any manifestation of it through rationality. The Sadducees were one of the many Jewish sects from biblical times, mainly aristocratic in origin and responsible for administrative matters. Their denial of an afterlife brought them into conflict with Christianity, hence Glanvill's need for a 'victory' over them. The book only appeared in its final form posthumously, although several editions were published during his lifetime.

Although Wiltshire is the setting for the first case in *Saducismus Triumphatus*, most of the others are concerned with incidents and occurrences in Somerset. These were mainly told to Glanvill by his friend Robert Hunt of Compton Pauncefoot, who, as well as being the Member of Parliament for Ilchester, was a Justice of the Peace and, like Glanvill, a fervent investigator of the paranormal. In his position as magistrate, Hunt had heard many cases alleged to involve the use of witchcraft or unnatural practices. The first of these to be included in the book by Glanvill recounts the story of Jane Brooks, a woman accused of witchcraft.

On the afternoon of Sunday 15 November 1657, 12-year-old Richard Jones was alone at his home in Shepton Mallet. His father, Henry, had left his son in perfect health, but on his return around an hour later, found the boy ill and in pain. It transpired, at least

Joseph Glanvill, vicar of Frome and author of Saducismus Truimphatus. (FSLS)

according to the boy, that during the time Jones senior was out, there had been a visitor to the house: Jane Brooks. Brooks lived in the same town and when she had called at the Jones' residence, she had asked for a piece of bread. In return, she gave the boy an apple and stroked his right side, before shaking his hand and bidding him 'good night'.

Richard Jones continued to experience pain in his right side during the night and the following evening. After roasting and eating the apple he had been given, he became extremely ill and, temporarily, lost the ability to talk. It was only after regaining the power of speech that he could tell his father about the visit from Jane Brooks (although he did not know her identity at that stage).

During the next period, Jones senior invited many of the town's womenfolk to see his son, hoping that the boy would recognise the one who had visited. Many women came over the course of the week, but it was on the following Sunday, when several were visiting, that the boy recognised Jane Brooks. Having given his father a sign – he had once more lost the power to verbally communicate – Jones senior approached Brooks and drew blood by scratching her face (a known way of lifting a witch's curse) and not long after, his son declared himself well again. It was, however, short-lived.

About a week after Henry Jones had drawn blood from Jane Brooks' face, Richard Jones met Alice Coward. The woman was Jane Brooks' sister and although the only thing that passed between them was her salutation of 'How do you do, my honey,' the boy soon became ill once more. Along with this illness came a vision of Brooks inside the house, being struck by a knife. On visiting Brooks' house, along with a constable, Richard's father found its occupant sitting on a stool with one hand covering the other. Unwilling to show the hidden hand, the constable forced the other off to reveal blood upon it – as if cut or scratched by a sharp instrument. The upshot of this was that Jane Brooks and Alice Coward appeared at Castle Cary before the local magistrates – Mr Hunt and the aptly named Mr Cary.

When Richard Jones was brought into the court for examination and saw the two women, he immediately became speechless. The next month, at Shepton Mallet, he again became mute on seeing Brook (although not Coward), while the following appearance, in front of various ministers, gentlemen and others, he fell into a fit within her presence and lay as if dead. Visions, toads croaking, and interior voices calling out the two women's names were just a few of the many manifestations of Richard Jones's 'illness', recorded

An imagined scene of the type of witches' covens Joseph Glanvill chronicled.

between the first and last court examinations; the result being that Jane Brooks stood trial as a witch at Chard Assizes on 26 March 1658. She was found guilty and executed not long afterwards.

What might be diagnosed in today's world as epilepsy, rather than the result of witchcraft was, at the time, enough for Hunt, and subsequently Glanvill, to 'prove' the existence of witches. 'This I think is good evidence of the being of witches,' Glanvill later wrote, and 'if the Sadducee be not satisfied with it, I would fain know what kind of proof he would expect.' This argument would also apply to the case of Elizabeth Style seven years later. As Andrew Pickering suggests, in his book *The Hellish Knot*, regarding this later case:

> *Elizabeth Style's case has many of the hallmarks of the classic English witch trial. She was accused by her neighbours of causing inexplicable sicknesses in her community ... [and her] victims*

included a child and another woman and, like Jane Brooks, she used the gift of an apple as an instrument of her maleficium. Once again the witch is visible to the bewitched child during her fits but invisible to others.

There is no doubt that Elizabeth Style of Stoke Trister was a 'witch', but the reality of the seventeenth century merely meant that she was a woman wise to the 'old ways' of herbal medicine, among other ancient traditions, with no interest in either worshipping the devil or cavorting naked in woods to celebrate the Sabbat. Nevertheless, she was charged with practising witchcraft and brought up in front of Robert Hunt, at Taunton, in 1664. Pickering recounts in his book, however, that even though the case had many of the classic witch-trial hallmarks, what set Style's case apart was the vivid description within her confession of 'meetings' with other (fully clothed) 'witches' and a handsome man in black. A 'confession' given, as Glanvill was quick to point out with great delight, 'free and unforced without any torturing'.

Although interpreted by Hunt and later Glanvill as devil-inspired Sabbats, another explanation for the meetings was merely the traditional gatherings and dances for specific holy days, attended by non-conformists driven to meet covertly by the Conventicle Act, which had come into being earlier that year. This Act (1664) was the third part of the Clarendon Code and forbade conventicles (a meeting for unauthorised worship) of more than five people who were not members of the same household. Therefore, it could be argued (and has been on several occasions) that the 'witches' were nothing more than members of a non-conformist congregation and the 'man in black' being no one more sinister than a minister such as John Humpfry, Glanvill's predecessor as Frome vicar, or any other clergymen who had lost their living after the Act of Uniformity.

Styles would more than likely have been found guilty of witchcraft and sentenced accordingly, based on various witness testimonies and indeed her own 'confession', but she escaped the hangman by dying in gaol before her execution. This does bring up an interesting point regarding the way convicted witches were executed. The popular image of 'trial by water' or being burned at the stake might fuel the imagination or be visually more 'entertaining' on screen, but the reality, at least in Somerset, was less fanciful. Most women found guilty of being a witch breathed their last at the end of a rope.

Although stake burning was an accepted alternate form of execution in many places outside Somerset, the practice of tying up a suspected witch and throwing her in a river to see if she would drown (meaning she was innocent) or float (meaning she was guilty and thus a candidate for execution) was illegal and only carried out by hastily assembled mobs. One such recipient of this form of rough justice was Margaret Waddam of Frome. The details are vague but what is known is that she survived her 'trial by water' by floating, but instead of being executed, successfully prosecuted three local vigilantes for attempted murder.

Possibly the most famous witchcraft case recorded in Joseph Glanvill's *Saducismus Triumphatus* is that of the Brewham witches. The Somerset civil parish of Brewham consists of two small villages – North and South – located east of Bruton and around nine miles south-west of Frome. Glanvill's account, again taken from testimonies given to Robert Hunt, detail the various misdeeds of several women and their victims, some of whom – participants and victims – were related to one another.

This coven of 'witches', as described by Glanvill, included Christine and Catherine Green (sisters-in-law), Margaret Agar and Mary Warberton. These women, along with others, would meet in Brewham Forest and while there, converse with the devil (or at least a man in black). Various ill-fortune or deaths would then befall members of the local community, considered to be the work of spells and other incantations practised by these women.

One example was the death of Catherine Green – mother-in-law to Christine and namesake Catherine – who, it was said, died in strange circumstances a few years earlier. Others who felt the wrath of the women included Jos Talbot and Richard Green; after falling out with one or other of the women, both had soon died, as witnesses would recount, through wax effigies of them being pierced by pins at late-night clandestine meetings. The fate which befell the 'Brewham' witches has been lost in time, apart from the gaol sentence handed out to Margaret Agar, which, given her main role in many of the effigy rituals, seems to be surprisingly light.

Joseph Glanvill's *Saducismus Triumphatus* is not just a compendium of witchcraft cases though, as other types of paranormal activities are recorded, including an account of poltergeist activity supposedly witnessed by the author himself.

John Mompesson, who lived in Tedworth (now Tidworth) in Wiltshire, became so incensed by the actions of an unlicensed drummer, one William Drury – whom he accused of collecting money by false pretences – that he brought a lawsuit against the vagrant. After winning the judgement, Drury's drum was turned over to the victor, but that was not the end of the story. Mompesson found himself plagued at night by the sound of drumming which, it was said, had been summoned by Drury. Glanvill himself visited Mompesson's house and while there, claimed to have heard scratching noises coming from under a bed in one of the children's rooms.

Another case involving a ghostly apparition was again the result of an interaction between two men, only this was one through the consensus of both parties. The men involved were Major George Sydenham, who lived in Dulverton, West Somerset and a near neighbour who lived in Skilgate, Captain William Dyke. The two engaged in endless conversations around the existence of God and the afterlife – Sydenham was a believer, Dyke was not – so they agreed, as in the best ghost stories, that whoever died first would visit the other on the third night following his funeral. In this way, the truth would be revealed once and for all.

As it transpired, the major went first and the captain, keen to see if his argument would hold up, duly kept a lookout for his erstwhile companion at the appointed time. When the major's ghost failed to turn up, Dyke felt vindicated in his views.

A few weeks later, however, while the captain was staying at an inn with a doctor friend, the 'wager' yielded another development. On the third day of his stay, he suddenly burst into the doctor's room 'in a visage and form much differing from himself, with his hair and eyes staring, and his whole body shaking and trembling,' as the doctor later recounted. One of the expressions that was used to describe Dyke's appearance was that he 'looked like he had seen a ghost' and, as it turned out, that is exactly what he had seen! As Dyke told his doctor friend, recalling his meeting with the ghost of his former neighbour, Major Sydenham: 'If ever I saw him in my life, I saw him now.'

The ghost had told him: 'I could not come at the time appointed, but I am now come to tell you that there is a God, and a very just and terrible one, as you will find if you do not turn over a new leaf!' According to Glanvill, Captain William Dyke took the ghost's words to heart: and from that day forward he was the model of a God-fearing man!

The first edition of *Saducismus Triumphatus* was published in 1666 and in this same year, Joseph Glanvill left Frome. He had accepted the position of Rector at Bath Abbey and the city would become his home for the rest of his life. He retained the living of Frome until 1672, when he exchanged it for that of Street. In the meantime, he also became Chaplin to King Charles II, seemingly shedding his previous, and now inconvenient, puritanism.

Richard Jenkins, who had held the living of Street until his deal with Glanvill, then became the latter's successor in Frome. During his time as vicar of St John's church, Jenkins officiated, in 1681, at the marriage ceremony of his patron Thomas Thynne (also known as Tom of Ten Thousand, due to the amount of revenue it was said he received from his estate at nearby Longleat) to Lady Ogle, the heiress to the Earl of Northumberland's vast wealth. The marriage did not last long, as Thynne was assassinated in Pall Mall the following year.

Joseph Glanvill died on 4 November 1680, aged 44 years, and was buried in Bath Abbey. *Saducismus Triumphatus* was published in its final version the following year, having been edited by Glanvill's close friend Henry More, although additional material regarding witchcraft in Sweden, supplied by Anthony Horneck, appeared in later editions.

It would not be an overstatement to say that Joseph Glanvill's *Saducismus Triumphatus* was one of the most important and influential books on witchcraft and the supernatural ever written – including its use as justification for a certain series of trials in seventeenth-century New England.

Six years before Joseph Glanvill was born, 700 Puritans had left English shores and sailed across the Atlantic to the newly founded Massachusetts Bay Colony. They had settled in various places around the bay area, included Salem. Twelve years after Glanvill died, the series of witchcraft trials that took place there and became the most infamous and notorious in history, began. Twenty people were executed; fourteen of whom were women and all but one was hanged. Five others (including two infant children) died in prison.

Those involved in the persecution of the alleged witches took as their justification, along with the relevant passages from the Bible, a book called *Memorable Providences*, written by Cotton Mathers, a New England Puritan minister. Mathers, in turn, cited his main inspiration and source for the book, as being Joseph Glanvill's *Saducismus Triumphatus*.

Although Glanvill did not stay long in Frome, the research and writings he undertook while there have given him a kind of immortality; however infamous.

Chapter 2

Eyes on the Crown

Frome and the Monmouth Rebellion, 1685

In many ways, the Monmouth Rebellion – the attempt by the Duke of Monmouth to seize the crown of England – could easily have ended in Frome in the final days of June 1685, rather than a week later and thirty miles down the road at Sedgemoor. Not that any battle was fought in the town, or indeed any major incident took place, it was just the factors that materialised elsewhere but reached Monmouth's ears during his three-day visit there might have caused a different outcome to the one history tells us.

James Scott, otherwise known as The Duke of Monmouth, was the acknowledged illegitimate son of Charles II and his mistress Lucy Walker. He was born in Rotterdam and was a soldier and protestant who tried to raise a rebellion against his uncle the Catholic James II.

On the 11 June 1685, he landed at Lyme Regis on England's south coast, with the intention of displacing the King and executing what he believed to be his divine right. From exile in Holland, Monmouth brought only eighty supporters with him, but throughout the rest of the month he travelled the West Country, recruiting large numbers of converts to his cause and fighting a series of skirmishes against the Royalist forces sent to defeat him.

Monmouth and his rebel army marched north to capture Bristol, but on reaching Keynsham were forced to retreat; the ragged band of farmers, artisans and labourers being no match for the regular army. It was then decided to head southeast, towards Wiltshire, with the intention of gathering even more recruits. They skirted the southern edges of Bath, before moving down towards the village of Norton St Philip, which they reached on Saturday 27 June 1685, and where Monmouth made temporary camp. Having rested, the rebels were preparing to leave for Frome, when the Royalist forces arrived on the outskirts of the village. A battle developed, in which Monmouth was allegedly shot through an upper window of the Old House (now The George Inn) while shaving, although he obviously survived – for now. In the end, it was the Royalist army who retreated, with Monmouth sitting on his white horse as he watched them go. Despite this victory, it was the beginning of the end.

The journey to Frome took place in the pouring rain, causing all manner of items to become sodden and soaked. They marched during the night and arrived in the town in the early morning. Notwithstanding their recent success, dissent was rife and it was a deflated and depressed band of rebels who arrived in the town on Sunday 28 June 1685.

Certain authors have suggested that Monmouth received an enthusiastic welcome from the townsfolk of Frome, but even if this was true, there was much to be depressed about; the most important aspect being the lack of arms and ammunition. A few days earlier, it had all seemed much brighter. While Monmouth was leading his army north from Shepton Mallet to Bristol, a small rebel detachment had been sent east to Frome. They arrived to find great excitement from the local population, with a large crowd gathering in the market place. The local constable, Robert Smith, read out Monmouth's proclamation and the rebel leader was declared King. One of the rebels – a man named Weely – then paraded through the town with several hundred men behind him; all carrying a variety of makeshift weapons, such as hatchets, pitchforks and clubs. This, however, was as good as it got for Monmouth in Frome.

There is a school of thought that suggests those locals who marched through the town carrying their weapons were in fact doing so because they believed the French had landed and were on their way from Bridgwater. Whatever the reason the populace came out in force, news of the rebel detachment's arrival in the town reached the Wiltshire militia, newly arrived in Bradford-on-Avon, and they swiftly made their way across the county border. Once there, they tore down the proclamation and arrested Constable Smith. Despite 'deeply regretting' his actions, he was reported to the Earl of Sunderland, who proclaimed that he should be 'hanged as he deserved' (as it turned out though, Smith was transported). The rest of the 'rabble' threw down their weapons – which were then seized by the militia – and begged for mercy.

On his arrival in Frome, Monmouth had made his headquarters in a house on Cork Street, the building later changing its name to Monmouth Chambers in honour of its 'royal' guest. Without arms, ammunition and other supplies though, the reluctance of many locals to join him and the lack of desertion he had expected from the King's forces, Monmouth fell into a state of deep depression.

Even so, the rebel leader was still gaining recruits here and there, and several came over from Longleat. The connection between the estate bordering the edges of Frome, and for many years in possession of large swathes of land within it, and the man who sought to be king, had been very strong. Five years earlier, in what became known as the Progress of 1680, Monmouth had travelled the West Country in a bid to gain supporters and friends who would legitimise his claim to the English throne after the death of his father, Charles II. One of those 'friends' he visited was Thomas Thynne, whose family ancestral home was the vast estate at Longleat.

Thomas Thynne, known as 'Tom of Ten Thousand' – due to the amount of money it was said he earned each year from his estate – had been the Duke of Monmouth's closest companion and on the last stop of his 'tour' – Longleat – he was welcomed by cheering

Longleat House, where the Duke of Monmouth was welcomed with a carpet of flowers, during his 'Royal Tour' of 1680. (Authors' Collection)

crowds at Rodden and then with a carpet of flowers on the actual estate. He even rode in the fateful coach with Thynne on the evening the latter was assassinated, but had alighted not long before the attack in Pall Mall; although he was back by the nobleman's side when he succumbed to his wounds at six the following morning.

Thomas Thynne's successor to Longleat – his cousin, also named Thomas – spent more of his time at Longleat, but was in London when Monmouth began his rebellion; leaving his estate in the hands of his wife, Frances and his steward, Thomas Allen. He was also more loyal to the king, and so left those at Longleat feeling somewhat afraid.

The connection between Monmouth and the late Thomas Thynne remained, however, in the shape of Captain James Kidd. Kidd had been the gamekeeper at Longleat and a long serving non-commissioned officer in the Wiltshire Militia, under the command of his employer, Thynne. When he moved almost permanently to London, Kidd had gone with him as steward. As Monmouth prepared for his campaign in Holland, the former Longleat employee joined him and was immediately given a captain's commission.

Now Monmouth and Kidd were in Frome, Longleat's present steward was anxious regarding the estate and Kidd's previous knowledge of it. According to Charles Trench in his classic book on the rebellion, *The Western Rising*: 'Allen expected daily that the rebels would search Longleat for horses and arms.' Allen, in fact, visited Frome and in a letter to his master, safely ensconced in London, he wrote:

> *They entered Frome yesterday at 4 in the morning very wett and weary. I believe they will march this day to Warminister, and call here as they goe. Capt. Kidd sent yesterday to T. Pierce desiring him to come to him. I went along with him, and found the Town full of armed men & horses, but cannot judge what number, unless I could see them drawn out the field. They report themselves to be 30,000, but if they be so many, the greatest part were asleep whilst I was there. The Duke rode round the town once in two houres, they call him King there as confidently as if he had the Crown on his head, and when they speak of his Majesty they call him York.*

There is no way of confirming the number of men with Monmouth while in Frome, but whether it was 3,000 or 30,000, most it seems were camped at Keyford, a separate parish to the south of the centre, and therefore perhaps not visible to Allen (although having said that, he would more than likely have passed through the parish on his way from and to Longleat). One fact seems to be confirmed though and that is, according to papers still preserved in the estate's archives, Captain Kidd acted as a recruiting agent in the area and may have enlisted as many as 500 to the cause.

On his first day in Frome, Monmouth's campaign took a further turn for the worse. He received news from Scotland that the rebellion there, led by the Earl of Argyll and in support of his own, had failed and his forces defeated (Argyll himself was captured and beheaded on Monmouth's last day in Frome, but he would not learn of his comrade's fate until later, if at all). The news of the defeat it is said, was 'a very great balk to him and gave a sudden damp to his spirits.'

The following day – Monday 29 June – Monmouth received another huge psychological blow. The King, James II, announced a pardon for all who had taken up arms, except a few named ringleaders, provided they surrendered to the king's troops or a magistrate within eight days. Many now, no doubt, began to feel the hopelessness of the situation and the call of home, of family, of the impending harvest, and regret for what they had done.

Monmouth was now in such depths of despair that he even proposed to a council of war that he, and several of his officers, should make their escape and return to Holland to regroup. It was at this point that he made the choice which might have changed history. There is no certainty that his return, better prepared, would have secured the crown, but we will never know because he was talked out of leaving and the path to Sedgemoor was laid.

On Monmouth's third and final day in Frome, he still had every intention of marching towards Warminster, to swell his army with the recruits said to be waiting for him there, and then onto his ultimate destination: London. The odds were now increasingly stacked up against him, as the Royalist forces, having learned of his intention, were quickly riding south to engage him. Not wanting an open confrontation on the Wiltshire plains, he ordered his army west and back towards Shepton Mallet. The Duke of Monmouth left Frome on Tuesday 30 June 1685, and within a little over a fortnight, he would be dead, having been defeated on the battlefield at Sedgemoor and then executed on London's Tower Hill for treason.

On the day that the Duke of Monmouth left Frome, the Earl of Feversham arrived, leading the Royalist troops. Although they had been told that all provisions had to be paid for, the troops 'pretty well plundered' the town. Nevertheless, when local man John Russell complained about £38 worth of hay that troops under Feversham's command had taken, the earl simply ordered the amount to be raised through the parish of Frome itself.

With the rebellion now quashed, it was time for retribution and it was swift, brutal and merciless. As well as Monmouth himself, many of the rebel officers were also executed, including Captain Kidd. He was captured and brought to the beach at Lyme Regis, where he had landed less than a month beforehand. Kidd was the last of twelve to be hanged and so witnessed the horrific spectacle of the other eleven men being dismembered before his eyes. Although naturally shaken to his core at this unimaginable horror, he pulled himself together and said a short prayer before his own turn.

The 'rank and file' of Monmouth's army, including many men from Frome who had not taken up the king's offer of clemency, would now play their part in one of the most infamous episodes in English judicial history: The Bloody Assizes.

Taunton Castle had been built to defend the town from which it took its name, and its history had already been long and bloody before the events of 1685. Its origins went back as far as Anglo-Saxon times, but it was the Normans in the twelfth century who built the stone-structured castle. A Great Hall was located on the first floor of the keep, over a stone vaulted under-croft and this was the setting for the series of trials in which Monmouth's supporters were tried for treason. More than 500 rebels were brought in front of the court over just two days – 18 and 19 September 1685 – and out of these, 144 were hanged, drawn and quartered; their remains then displayed around the county so people understood the fate of those who rebelled against the king. The rest of the rebels were transported to the Americas.

If these assizes became notorious, then so did the judge who presided over them. Lord Chief Justice Jeffreys was the 40-year-old, Welsh-born judge who, through his merciless and harsh sentencing at these trials, became known to history as 'The Hanging Judge'.

According to W.M. Wigfield, in his exhaustively researched book *The Monmouth Rebels'* more than fifty Frome men stood trial, with many others from neighbouring villages and

An old postcard showing Taunton Castle, the scene of Bloody Assizes in 1685. (Authors' Collection)

outlying parishes, such as Beckington, Bruton, Marston Bigot, Mells, Rode, Rodden, Whatley and Witham Friary. These were the blacksmiths, card-makers, carpenters, chandlers, coopers, clothworkers, felt-makers, glaziers, masons, weavers, wiredrawers, woodsman, and yeomen of the area who had taken up arms – often the tools of their trade – and embarked on what was meant to be a glorious rebellion. For many, their reward was death or deportation. Among those transported to the Americas included Humphrey Davys and Henry Symes, both yeomen from Frome who were transported on the *Port Royal Merchant* to Jamaica, leaving England towards the end of October 1685, and Stephen Rodway and Richard Wadham, whose journey from Bristol to Barbados took place onboard the *John*. Like many of their comrades, the latter two had been sold as slaves to plantation owners out there. In this case, Rodway and Wadham was sold to Ann Gallup and Colonel John Sampson, respectively.

Although not from Frome, twelve rebels were hanged on Gibbet Hill. Although not originally from the town, it was an act replicated in many places throughout Somerset with the intention of quelling any further acts of rebellion. The men were Robert Beaumont, William Clement, John Humphreys, George Hussey, Laurence and Thomas Lott, Robert Man, Thomas Paull, Francis Smith, Philip Usher, Samuel Vile, and Thomas Warr. They were hanged, drawn and quartered; with their remains being hung at Gorehedge, where Keyford joins The Butts and where the Fire Station is located today. Contrary to local folklore, Gorehedge was already known as such before the hangings, rather than after them, having gained its name from the gorse that once grew there.

Chapter 3

I, Daniel Neale

The illustrious career of Frome's very own highwayman, 1763

The second half of the eighteenth century is seen today as the golden age of the 'Gentleman Rogues' – when men (and less often women) would ride upon their trusty steeds and roam the highways and byways of the rapidly expanding road system to rob stagecoaches and other travellers.

These highwaymen achieved a romantic reputation conjuring up images of a masked individual, bedecked in cloak and three-cornered hat, armed with blunderbusses and robbing unfortunate victims with the familiar cry of 'stand and deliver', while at the same time, charming their lady companions.

The reality, however, was often very different and during this period those who were operating as highwaymen were more likely to be cold-blooded cutthroats, callous killers or just plain rogues, without any gentlemanly qualities attached. They mainly came from the ranks of the lower classes and lacked the sophistication of their more idealised predecessors; dispossessed nobles who had taken to highway robbery out of desperation following the end of the English Civil War.

Many areas in Somerset, as in other counties, had at least one infamous participator and the town of Frome was no different; although this highwayman, along with the gang he assembled, were not foolish enough to ply their trade too near 'home', choosing instead to operate in another county altogether: that of Gloucestershire.

From what can be ascertained, more than 350 years after the fact, it seems more than likely that the man who became Frome's own self-styled 'gentleman of the road' was born Daniel Neal in 1742 – but not in the town. His parents, Francis and Sarah Neal, lived in Horsley, a Gloucestershire village near the town of Nailsworth.

Frome had its very own highwayman in the shape of Daniel Neale.

How Neal ended up in Frome is not known, if it is the same person, but there is a possibility it was through marriage. Both Neal's parents and those of his future wife – the Harris family – were in the cloth trade and it is possible that it was an 'arranged' marriage to strengthen the two businesses. Whatever the reason, marriage records for Frome Selwood show a Daniel Neal marrying an Anne Harris on 11 June 1758. The groom was recorded as being 16 years of age, which would fit with a 1742 birthdate. If the marriage was 'arranged' then the fact he was over the age of 14 – the legal age at which a man could marry without parental consent – was immaterial. The same could be said of the bride: with the female legal age set at 12 and the bride being 13. How the businesses benefited we do not know, but the union produced at least one child – a girl the couple named Sarah and christened in Frome on 9 January, 1762.

The clothing connection seems viable enough, as court reports would later detail the fact that Daniel Neale (the 'e' suffix added by either by Daniel himself at some point, or else a misprint by the newspapers) lived in Frome with his wife, where he 'worked at the clothing business'. His wife, it was reported, owned the shop (or possibly her parents did and she ran it for them).

What motivated Daniel Neale, as we shall call him from here on in, to enter the nefarious profession of highway robbery, we shall never know – perhaps his wife's business wasn't going well, even though the woollen industry in Frome was in its heyday – but by the summer of 1763, he had regularly begun to borrow a mare from the landlord, Joseph Mintrim, of the Black Swan in Bridge Street. His 'cover' story involved 'going on journeys for gentlemen', connected with his wife's clothing business. He would be away for anything up to a fortnight at a time.

His 'business trips' must have been lucrative, as one newspaper article would later report that Neale would show watches and considerable amounts of money to his shop mates – at his wife's shop, it is presumed – saying that there were far easier ways of making money than working.

The little we know of Frome's highwayman begins with a report in the *Gloucester Journal* for Monday 4 July 1763:

> *We have received the following particulars of a most audacious villain that has this week infested the roads between this place and Bath. On Wednesday morning* [29 June] *he attacked, near the monument at Lansdown, two persons whom he robbed of some small sums, and afterwards coming to the turnpike on this side of the down, he found there a man who was paying for passing through, on which the highwayman ordered the turnpike man to go into his house and shut the door, or he would blow his brains out, saying 'I'll receive this gentleman's money' and accordingly robbed the person of a considerable sum. He then came on to a little ale-house on the cross road, where he put up his horse and staid half an hour, and having drunk a quart of strong beer, and fed his horse, he told the landlord he should set off for Tetbury.*
>
> *Upon the road near Petty France he robbed a gentleman's servant of eight guineas, and soon after, meeting with a man returning from Tetbury market, near Dunkirk, he demanded his money. The man, who had a little boy before him, told the villain that he had none. He then demanded his watch, and endeavoured to pull it out of his pocket by the string, which in the struggle broke, and the man refusing to give it him, he said, 'Do you contest with me?', and he immediately putting his pistol over the boy's shoulder, fired it, and lodged three slugs in the poor man's breast, of which he died soon after. The villain was*

> *immediately pursued by some people who heard the report of the pistol, but he got away.*
>
> *The Landlord of the house where he baited says he is a short young man, about 18, pitted much with the small pox, well-mounted on a dark brown mare, which is blind of one eye, and has a switch tail. One of his stirrups is new, the other is an old one.*

A report in the *Bath Chronicle* of 7 July, however, gives a slightly different account of the day:

> *a Highwayman stopped a butter-woman on Lansdown … and robbed her of a guinea and a half and some silver; likewise robbed a collier of three shillings and six-pence. Soon after he stopped a gentleman's servant at Toghill turnpike and robbed him of about 5 shillings … a few miles further he overtook another gentleman's servant with whom he travelled to Petty France where they baited* [fed] *their horses and afterwards set out together but at the parting of the Gloucester and Tetbury Roads the Highwayman stopped the servant and presenting a pistol to his breast robbed him of about five guineas and his watch threatening if he did not return the same road he came he would shoot him.*
>
> *The servant returned to the inn and requested the landlord to assist him in pursuit of the villain, he being gone the Gloucester road; which he immediately did and they pursued him close as to come within 200 yards of him but he seeing them leaped his horse over a stone wall and escaped.*
>
> *While the servant was returning to the inn the villain attacked a Pig killer of Wickwar who keeps the sign of The Crown there and on demanding his money the man told him he had but 4/6d, on which the Highwayman demanded his watch but he not giving it directly the villain seized on the chain and seals and forced it from the watch; then telling him he was an obstinate dog drew a pistol from under his coat and firing at him lodged five slugs in his right breast. He is not yet dead,* [as has been reported] *but tis thought he cannot recover.*

It was almost a month later that the perpetrator was caught and his identity revealed, as this item from the *Gloucester Journal* for Monday 25 July 1763, reported:-

On Saturday last, (23 July) about noon, a man came to a blacksmith's shop in Chalford Bottom, to have his horse shod. Some people who happened to be present thought he exactly answered the description which we gave in this paper of the highwayman who shot the man upon the Bath road about three weeks ago. They then surveyed his mare and found that also to correspond with an account of it upon which they immediately seized him, and in his pockets found a brace of pistols loaded with gravel stones and bits of lead, which confirming their suspicions, they carried him directly before a justice, who committed him to the care of the constable, by whom he was secured at the George at Bisley.

The noise of the highwayman being taken brought many people to see him and amongst the rest a man who had been robbed near Cirencester that morning. This person coming into the room where the highwayman was at supper, immediately declared that he was the fellow who had robbed him in the morning. 'And will you swear to that?' said the highwayman. To which the other replied in the affirmative. 'Why then' says the villain, 'I may as well die first as last', and with the knife with which he was eating his supper cut his throat in a shocking manner. He was not dead yesterday morning, but it was thought he could not live till night. He has committed many robberies between Cirencester, Malmsbury, and Tetbury and had in his pocket when taken away, about eight guineas. It is very fortunate this desperado is apprehended, as it is imagined he was crossing over to intercept the traders on their road to Bristol fair.

On 28 July 1763, the *Bath Chronicle* added that the man was thought to have been a member of the Gloucestershire militia and that his horse was stolen. The article also named the victim of the turnpike robbery as Mr Rutter of Cirencester who was robbed of 3 guineas and his watch.

Neale recovered from his injuries and stood trial at the Gloucester Assizes which took place during August. He was charged with three robberies, those at Lansdown, Toghill, Petty France and the murder of the pig killer/landlord at Dunkirk. The *Gloucester Journal* 22 August 1763 reported that:

Neale, the highwayman, relates that he launched forth into this scene of villainy a few weeks before Easter last, with two accomplices, whose names he will not discover, but acknowledges

> *that they live near Frome. He says it was to supply themselves with cash for the cockpit and the ale-house that they took to the highway, and that they have committed many robberies. Cutting cloth from clothiers' racks was another part of their employ, as the inhabitants of Shepton Mallet have experienced to their cost. He confesses that they had formed a grand scheme of robbery to be carried into execution as soon as good horses* [and] *pistols … could be procured, and to elude circumstantial descriptions of their persons, they had concluded in the following stratagem, to meet every night at a certain rendezvous, and there change each other's cloths, horses etc. The conviction of this enterprising villain is, therefore a most fortunate event for this and the neighbouring counties. The execution … is fixed for Friday.*

What might have seemed a cunning plan initially, borrowing a horse in Frome and travelling all the way to Gloucestershire to commit his crimes, seems to have contributed greatly to his undoing. Apart from his short stature and pock-marked face, the one-eyed mare with a false tail is what the victims remembered most about their assailant and he was 'convicted on the evidence of the gentleman's servant whom he robbed just before he shot the butcher'; presumably the same servant with whom he had been eating, drinking and travelling before deciding to rob him. His admission that the money was to provide cash for the 'cockpit and the ale-house', was not much in the way of mitigation and on 10 August 1763, at the end of the court session, he was convicted and sentenced to death.

He was hanged at the village of Over two miles west of Gloucester on Friday 26 August, along with Richard Johnson a housebreaker. This village was the county execution site until 1792, and the condemned men were said to have been conveyed to the gallows in carts, sitting on their own coffins.

The *Bath Chronicle* for 1 September 1763 reports that the housebreaker Johnson,

> *went to the gallows in his shroud and in his whole behaviour evinced the sincerest penitence and resignation to his fate. When the executioner put the rope around his neck he exclaimed with great fervour, 'Welcome Halter!' Neale expressed great terror at the approach of death and seemed to think that his sins had been too great to be expiated by so short a repentance; and prolonged the moment in which he was to be turned off to the very last.*

Why someone so young and established in business with a wife and daughter should embark on such a drastic course we can only guess at. Drink? Gambling? Or just youthful bravado? We will never know; unless, as he told his work colleague, it was simply that he believed there were far easier ways of making money than working. If this was the case, then Daniel Neale paid the ultimate price for his belief.

Chapter 4

Slaughter in the Market Place

John Crees and The Blue Boar, 1823

In the early hours of a Sunday morning in March 2017, an affray occurred in a Frome pub. The incident at the public house, located in the town centre, seemingly began with a slap on a female drinker's bottom, by a fellow (male) customer. On complaining to her 'assailant', the woman was told in no uncertain terms, by another member of the perpetrator's group that it was, in fact, her own fault she had been slapped because she 'shouldn't have such a big arse'. Unsurprisingly, the woman's husband confronted the group of males and an altercation ensued. The case and those involved in it ended up in court.

The outcome of this 'silly incident', so called by the defending solicitor, was that his client felt apologetic and was disgusted at his own alcohol-fuelled behaviour. Despite this remorse, the judge sentenced him to an eighteen-month community order with 180 hours unpaid work and a twenty-five-day Rehabilitation Activity Requirement. He was also ordered to pay £135 compensation to the victims along with £85 costs and an £85 victim surcharge.

There have been many public houses and inns in and around the market town of Frome that have acquired reputations for rowdy behaviour and violent clashes, but perhaps none so much as The Blue Boar in the town's Market Place. The fact that it is still serving after more than three centuries is testament to its popularity, although judging from the above incident in the twenty-first century, it seems that its reputation is still intact.

The long history of The Blue Boar is no doubt filled with such 'silly incidents' as that mentioned above. It was built at the end of the seventeenth century by Theophilus Lacey, a mercer, following a lease granted to him for ninety-nine years on 3 November 1691.

The Blue Boar, witness to various nefarious incidents over the centuries, including the manslaughter of John Crees in 1823. (Authors' Collection)

It is uncertain when The Blue Boar began to acquire its notorious reputation, but certainly by the late eighteenth century the foundations had been laid. In 1771, for example, the landlady, Elizabeth Bedbury, found herself up in front of the magistrates after she had taken the hat of a male customer and refused to return it to him. He took out a summons against her and despite her plea that the customer had 'acted insolently' towards her, the magistrate ordered her to 'hand it back'. The following year, 1772, it was the turn of her husband to find himself on the wrong end of a tongue-lashing by a local magistrate. Appearing, supposedly as a witness, in the court case concerning the assault of two customers by an army sergeant, Bedbury found himself being reprimanded for 'not being so active as he should have been' in suppressing the disturbance.

By the early nineteenth century, trouble seemed to follow The Blue Boar like a dog after a bone. When Isaac Gregory kept diaries of his time as the local constable in Frome, the pub's name cropped up in several entries. On one occasion, in March 1818, when the 40-year-old law officer was called to the pub, he was in no mood for petty squabbles, later recording in his diary that he had been 'sent for in haste to The Blue Boar 2 men was fighting in the parlour one of the men lost his hat and had his clothes much torn, it served him right as he had no business there and he had no pity from me'. Two months earlier, Gregory had taken 'a person into custody by the name of Wilkins for passing a bad half Guinea and refusing to change it – Searched him at the Blue Boar and found a very bad shilling in his Pockets.' When a fair was on, and a 'great muster of pickpockets' had come over from Bristol, various purses were stolen, with an empty double purse being found at The Blue Boar.

For those disagreements over the centuries where the actual fighting didn't take place on the premises, the alcohol drunk there fuelled the various affrays that kicked off in the Market Place outside. One example, according to Gregory, took place on a market day, with 'a severe battle for a long continuance in the lower Market'. It seemed the farmers enjoyed it so much, he would later learn from one of the market women, that no one would send for him. Finally, when he did arrive, he discovered the cause of this market day 'battle' to have been a passing farmer striking another's cow on the horn. 'Very serious things often arise from trifling causes – the above is an instance of it,' was Isaac Gregory's opinion of the matter.

Another time, the chief constable was called,

> *late at night to quell a dangerous and vicious fight in the Market Place. They was* [*sic*] *fighting and kicking down as well as up till I parted them. I never saw a more deplorable object than one of them looked. He did not look like a human being – he was so completely covered with mud and blood.*

The cause of this altercation has been lost in time but five years later, with Gregory long since returned full-time to his currier business in Cheap Street, another fight broke out whose outcome was more tragic, but whose ignition, or at least the spark of it, can be traced within the walls of the public house.

On Saturday 23 August 1823, Francis Singer, a labourer, walked into The Blue Boar and met his friends John Crees and brother George. The pair from Hemington, located between

Frome and Bath, had just been to the latter to buy two reap hooks, or sickles, and whose extremely sharp edges were bound up with straw for protection. Singer sat down and drank a pint of beer with them. On the other side of the room was another group of

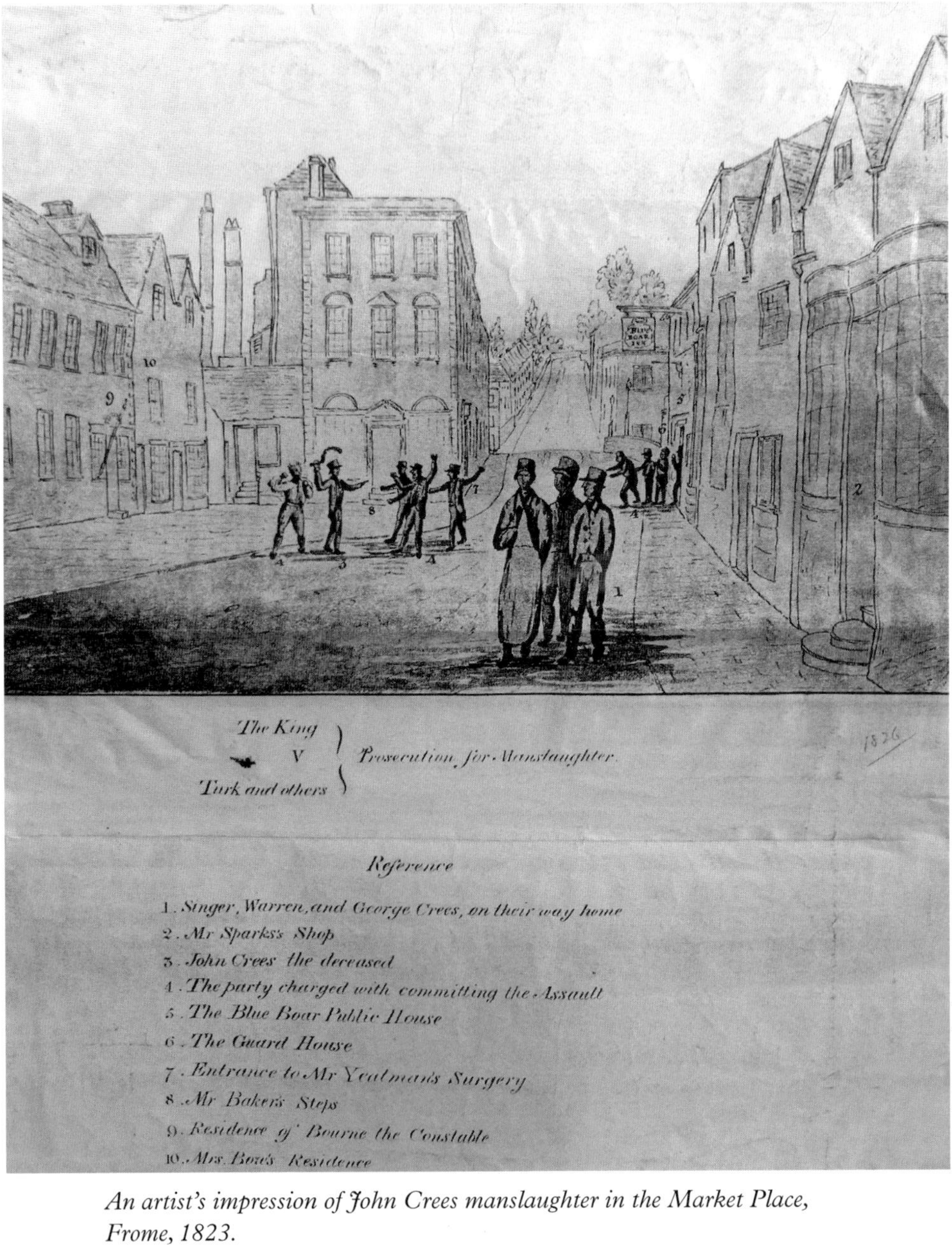

An artist's impression of John Crees manslaughter in the Market Place, Frome, 1823.

friends drinking together, 19-year-old Thomas Adams, 17-year-old Timothy Turk and John Richards, who was 24 years old.

A man named Coombs came in and ordered a pint. He drank some of it and left the rest while he went to the toilet. During the time Coombs was absent, it seems Timothy Turk grabbed his pint and drank the remainder of it. When Coombs returned and asked what had happened to his drink, Turk's group denied all knowledge of it.

There is some suggestion that words were exchanged between Turk and Singer's group at some point, but this cannot be substantiated, as no transcripts of the inquest or trial can be found and surviving newspaper reports give a confused picture. It may be assumed that Coombs, the man whose pint was stolen, was a friend of either Singer and or the Crees brothers, although he does not appear in the story after this incident, which seems to have sparked off later events.

During the evening, Francis Singer and the Crees were joined by a Samuel Warren. George Crees, Warren and Singer then left the pub at about 10 o'clock at night. They had only walked a short distance when they heard whooping and shouting behind. They turned around and saw John Crees, who had been a little behind his companions in leaving, waving the now unsheathed reap hook around and defending himself against an attack by six or so men, including Thomas Adams and Timothy Turk. The men also loudly challenged John Crees's brother, George, and the others with him, to come back and fight them. Warren heard one of the prisoners say: 'I'll give you a bellyful', along with much cursing and swearing at his party.

John Crees was then set upon and an affray began. Despite being the only one in possession of a weapon, he was overpowered and knocked to the ground by a blow to the head from Thomas Adams. Once on the ground, the 19-year-old Adams again punched him. Crees dropped the reap hook and John Richmond picked it up.

Before he was hit, Crees must have inflicted some damage on his opponents, as Timothy Turk left the scene almost immediately, saying one of his hips had been cut. The others then no doubt fled. The unconscious John Crees was picked up by the alerted police and taken to the guardhouse, next door to The Blue Boar.

The guardhouse was built in 1724 and although it had undoubtedly been erected in this location for its proximity to the Magistrates' Court, which at that time was just diagonally across the bridge, down Bridge Street a few yards and then left to the end of Edgell's Lane (today known as Justice Lane), it was perhaps ironic that it was also situated exactly next door to The Blue Boar; a coincidence that only enhanced its less than salubrious reputation.

In 1851, almost thirty years after John Crees was taken there, two of the four men – William Maggs and William Sergeant – who appeared in front of magistrates charged with the brutal killing of 14-year-old Sarah Watts, were arrested at the same pub by Detective Sergeant Smith and hastily locked up next door. How many others, over the centuries, shared the same fate of drinking in the pub one minute and staring at the bare guardhouse walls the next? The building became redundant six years later, in 1857, when the new police station – complete with cells – came into operation in Christchurch Street West. It later became a ladies' toilet, before finally being demolished in the 1960s.

When John Crees was involuntarily put into the guardhouse, near the end of August 1823, the seriousness of his injuries was not recognised; the surgeons apprentice in attendance was merely informed that Crees was drunk and so did not bother to examine him in any detail.

Samuel Bourne the constable did not know that Crees had received a blow to the head until he saw him the next morning bleeding from the nose and insensible. The surgeon was called and ordered his immediate removal to a private house, where Crees lingered on in great pain before dying from his injuries the following Wednesday. Francis Bush, the surgeon, later deposed that he had no doubt the deceased died in consequence to having received a blow to the head. After his death, he opened Crees's skull and found the brain 'much inflamed'.

Five young men were arrested and charged with manslaughter. The men were Thomas Adams – 19, Timothy Turk – 17 and John Richards – 24, who had all been present when the initial provocation – the drinking of Coombes' pint – had taken place, along with two others, Edward Noble – 16 and 15-year-old Charles Snelgrove.

The *Bath Chronicle*'s report of the magistrates' court case said that coroner Peter Laying had conducted 'A most minute investigation, which occupied two days was entered into before the coroner and his jury and no pains were spared to elucidate all the circumstances of the case by a long examination of more than twenty witnesses.'

Magistrates were appointed by the Crown for each county and were, for the most part, gentlemen who owned or occupied land to the value of at least £100 a year. As the position was unpaid, it meant magistrates were largely from the middle class or above, and often local employers or professionals. They were normally unqualified layman, but supposedly educated enough to listen to cases and dispense justice impartially. A magistrate was entitled to sit in any part of the county but, in practice, tended to remain local.

If the case was of a lesser degree the magistrates could try it themselves. If the charge was more serious, known as 'indictable', they conducted a preliminary investigation to establish that it was a reasonable one. This included hearing evidence from police and several principle witnesses. As this crime was manslaughter, the latter applied. Once brought before the court, Adams, Turk and the others, would have the charges read out to them and then be asked for their plea – 'guilty' or 'not guilty'. If they answered with the latter, the magistrates would invite the prosecution to call evidence from witnesses, including the arresting officer, in support of its case. The accused – or their representative – would then have the chance to call their own witnesses in rebuttal. In this case all the accused pleaded not guilty

As the magistrates were mostly laymen, they were assisted in matters of law by an appointed clerk. In Frome, this was from the firm of solicitors Wickham & Cruttwell. Their offices were in Bath Street, the large thoroughfare cut in 1810 to the south of the town centre. They also occupied a building at the end of Edgell's Lane, where the market car park now stands, but which was used as the magistrate's court. It was not uncommon in many parts of the county, at least until the introduction of a specific Act in 1849, for cases to be heard in the private house of one of the bench, a hired room or even in a public house like the inquests – so Frome was fortunate in having its own court a long time before that.

Eventually, after a long deliberation, the jury returned a verdict of manslaughter against Turk, Adams and Noble as principals, and against John Richmond and Charles Snelgrove as aiders and abetters. They were all committed by the coroner to Ilchester Gaol for trial at the next Assize.

The trial duly took place and at the end of it, the judge summed up the evidence and explained to the jury that as no previous malice could be shown on behalf of the prisoners, and that the circumstances were very confused, they should be very cautious in drawing the line of demarcation as to the guilt of each of the individual prisoners.

The jury, 'consisting of 16 most respectable gentlemen', consulted for some time and returned a verdict of 'Guilty' against Adams, and 'Not Guilty' as to the rest of the prisoners. The 19-year-old Thomas Adams was sentenced to four months imprisonment in Ilchester Gaol.

Chapter 5

Most Extraordinary Depredators

The escapades of the burglarious Howarth Brothers, 1827

In the early hours of Monday 6 August 1827, two lads were returning to their lodgings adjoining the cooperage of Joseph Oxley at Frome when they observed three men. One was inside the timber house, while the other two stood guard outside. Bravely, the two lads approached the men, who then ran off. The pair woke the owner of the timber house, Joseph Oxley, who grabbed a lantern and carving knife. The trio made their way back to the wood store, where they found its door had been broken open and a large amount of timber had been stacked outside ready to be carted away.

The night was almost pitch black and it was assumed the would-be thieves had fled, but then one of the searchers heard a rustling in the garden next door. Without hesitation, Joseph Oxley jumped over the adjoining fence and after a brief search, with lantern in hand, discovered a very powerful, ill-looking fellow secreted among the bushes, with a drawn sword in his hand. The man attempted to escape, cutting backwards with his sword, but was instantly pursued. Having overtaken the villain, Oxley got the man backed up against a fence. A fight ensued in which Oxley was stabbed in the side and received a tremendous blow to the head, but he fought back. The handle of the lantern held by Oxley became twisted and he was temporarily prevented from using his left hand to grapple with the man. Eventually though, he managed to discard it and fought on, sword against carving knife, until his opponent cried for mercy and threw down his weapon.

Oxley took the criminal to the guard house in the town centre, where he was searched and discovered to be in possession of

The rear of The Blue Boar, where a handcuffed George Howarth leapt to freedom. (Authors' Collection)

a dark lantern, tinder box and steel, tin candle box, disguising cap and a large knife; all looking as though they had been in use for many years. The sword was about 2ft long, and sewn into the fustian jacket was a pocket contrived for holding the lantern. After this search, the injured man was taken to The Blue Boar public house, which stood next to the guardhouse in Frome market place, where his wounds were attended to.

While upstairs in the pub, the handcuffed captive managed to get his 5ft 10in tall frame through an upstairs window and leapt from a height of around 20ft into the River Frome below. After a brisk journey across the swiftly flowing water, a still manacled villain scrambled up onto the opposite bank to freedom. Over the next few days, more than two hundred locals scoured the area, but even when joined by a Bow Street Runner from London and a reward of 100 guineas, their search was to no avail.

Despite the authorities no longer having the physical body of the criminal, they did have his identity and the story which unfolded was one of the most incredible, and almost unbelievable, in the annals of Frome history. What Joseph Oxley did not know when he confronted the man who had attempted to rob his timber house was that he had just ended an incredible spree of burglaries spread over decades – and the burgler was the last person anyone would have suspected.

George Howarth was a pillar of the community. He was born around 1782 in the village of Mobberely, near Knutsford in Cheshire, but had lived in Frome for the past sixteen years. His occupation was a millwright and he lived with his wife and children in the Old Nunnery in Keyford, an area due south of the town centre that had once been a separate parish, but was now amalgamated into Frome.

The local constabulary made their way out to Howarth's house and began a search of the premises. What they found can

The Old Nunnery, Lower Keyford, where the Howarth brothers hid a huge stash of stolen goods. (Authors' Collection)

only be described as an Aladdin's cave; with stolen items of every description that included dresses, books, gunpowder, bullets, stove grates, a dog house, iron bars, numerous gardening and labouring tools, earthenware, sets of scales, new timber boards, chains, bags of hops, casks and velvet pulpit cloths and cushions. The latter two items, it transpired, had been stolen from one of Frome's churches six years earlier. Among this haul was a bag formerly used for containing parish money. The bag had been under the care of a respectable man, but after it was stolen he was falsely accused (it was now realised) of stealing it and died of a broken heart over the ordeal.

Further detailed examination of the Old Nunnery revealed yet more surprises secreted in the most extraordinary manner, mainly below floorboards and in large recesses under the roof that had been plastered over. Among the latest treasure trove recovered from inside these hidden recesses were nearly 200yds of fine cloth, several blankets stolen from the parish blanket manufactory, curiously contrived swords for wearing under one's trousers, a quantity of cooper's timber (obviously stolen on a previous occasion from Mr Oxley's premises) carpets, sheepskins and skeleton keys.

The physical attributes of George Howarth's life of crime were there for all to see, but more was to come to light through his wife. When it was announced to her that he had escaped from The Blue Boar, she boasted with pride that her husband had eluded capture in the same manner many times. Her tale was reported in the *Bath Chronicle* for 30 August 1827: 'About 22 years ago he escaped from Middlewich Gaol,' she had recounted to a reporter, 'and was hotly pursued by the police of Manchester'. Howarth managed to escape into a wood 'where he remained for a month and subsisted on wheat and milk'. On a similar occasion, he escaped into a wood and was not found even though the area was scoured by three regiments of soldiers; some of whom were within a few yards of him. His wife even had a nickname for him – 'The Stag' – through his dexterity at eluding these hunters.

As for his most recent escape, from The Blue Boar, George had employed a similar strategy. After scrambling up the banks of the River Frome and onto terra firma once more, he had made his way through fields and lanes to a barn almost three miles from Frome, where he remained until the following evening. While there, he managed to rid himself of his handcuffs, by bashing them repetitively with a stone until they broke. He had then returned to his house in Frome, but finding constables in attendance he remained in a cowshed adjoining it until the early hours, when he started for the woods near Longleat, where he remained for the next few days. During this time, he was spotted at Stourhead, about ten miles to the south of Frome, but eluded those pursuing him. He was next seen at Pen Pitts Woods near Bourton, in Dorset, four miles further south.

According to reports on the latest sighting at Pen Pitts,

> [Howarth] *called at a lonely cottage by the wood in a near exhausted state one day last week and entreated the woman who occupies it to bring him some water. At that moment, he saw a person on horseback coming up the lane close by and immediately fell flat in the ditch until the person had passed; he then crossed into the wood in a very weak state and beckoned to the cottager to bring the water to him. She became alarmed at his extraordinary appearance and hesitated for some time what to do, but never having heard of Howarth's depredations, nor anything relative to the recent transactions which have rendered him so notorious, she charitably placed a jug of water within a short distance of him.*

When the woman came back to retrieve the jug, Howarth was gone. The newspaper report ended by suggesting that although

> [the] *pursuit is still going on and although the miserable fugitive is in that part of the ancient forest of Selwood where he can travel for nearly ten miles still in his exhausted state, want of food and clothing must prevent his proceeding much further without being apprehended, especially as hand bills offering 100 guineas reward and giving a full description of his person have been carefully delivered to every cottager in the neighbourhood.*

Given the above, what happened next must be ranked as truly extraordinary and a most incredible feat of endurance. Perhaps realising that he could no longer stay in the local area without the imminent risk of capture, George Howarth decided to head north and back to the place of his birth, a journey of nearly 200 miles, which he undertook by travelling at night and hiding in the woods or plantations he encountered on his route during daylight hours. To further hamper his progress, he had an imperfectly cured fracture on his left leg just above his ankle from a previous injury that had not healed properly; this not only made that leg crooked, but also slowed his gait. On the plus side though, his feet were very large and he was described as of 'strong muscular form'.

When he came through Bath, he stayed in the woods surrounding Prior Park – the one-time residence of Ralph Allen – before skirting around the fringes of the city to reach the beginning of the Gloucester Road. He then carried on north, passing through Gloucester, Birmingham and Stoke-on-Trent, before finally reaching the village of his birth and, what he hoped would be, the sanctuary of his brother's house. He was, however, 'in a dreadful state of exhaustion owing to loss of blood from the wounds inflicted by Mr Oxley in the struggle and from the fatigue of travelling.' If one brother was taking a lot of risk for harbouring his fugitive sibling, back in Frome another had already felt the full weight of the law.

Not long after George Howarth's house had been visited, the local constables and magistrates paid a visit to that of his younger brother, Ralph. The two brothers had lived together with their respective families at the Old Nunnery until four years beforehand. Ralph had moved out and rented another place nearby (it was later said that it was possibly due to the amount of space being taken up by all the stolen merchandise). When the local law officers entered the premises, another large haul of ill-gotten gains was discovered. If not as great a haul as that at the Old Nunnery – there had been many more years to fill the nooks and crannies there – the revelation of what was found shocked all those who knew him. If George Howarth had been an outwardly respectable member of the Frome community, then his brother, Ralph, was even more so. He was a master millwright and member of the Methodist Church but, nonetheless, he was arrested by the constables, along with his two sons.

A report in the *London Evening Standard* seemed to sum up the feelings of the local population:

> *It is extraordinary … that he [George] and his brother [Ralph] should have so long continued their unparalleled depredations in Frome and the neighbourhood without even once exciting the smallest suspicion. It is acknowledged by their wives that for the past 16 years they have been constantly in the practice of all kinds of robberies, from sacrilege, burglary, and sheep stealing down to petty garden thefts. George's wife sold vegetables and*

> *fruit which were supplied by the latter means and she actually wore a pelisse made from the communion table cloth stolen from Christ Church about 6 years ago.*

The paper revealed some of the hazards the brothers had overcome, as it reported that George had been fired on at least six times within the last seven months.

The 49-year-old Ralph Howarth was sentenced at the Bridgwater Assizes, in August 1827, to two terms of seven years transportation for stealing a gun and a sack from William Baily in Frome, along with other items. His sons Robert – 23, and Isaac – 17, were released because there was no direct evidence against them, even though goods were found beneath the floorboards of their room. One of the indictments against Ralph was the theft of a gig, the property of Lewis Drews, a painter and glazier of Frome. The story goes that the day after the theft, he and George went to Drews's shop and purchased paint from him so they could repaint his gig to disguise it!

During Ralph's arrest and subsequent court appearance, George Howarth had managed to evade capture, but by the time he was sent to the prison hulk *Captivity*, anchored at Devonport, in September 1827 to await transportation to Australia, his brother had been re-captured and taken to Knutsford Gaol. Ralph was to spend two years on the rotting hulk before being bundled aboard the *Claudine* and dispatched to New South Wales to serve his fourteen years.

In the end, after such an incredible undertaking, it was a series of unfortunate incidents and just sheer bad luck that saw George Howarth apprehended on Sunday, 2 September. The first of these concerned a Mr Whitehead. He was an overseer in Frome and like most of the population in the town, became familiar with George's earlier escape from Middlewich Gaol in Cheshire (where the height from which he leapt to freedom, so it was said, not only doubled that of The Blue Boar jump but it was onto solid ground, rather than water.) It was this connection with the fugitive's path that led Whitehead to send one of the printed leaflets, offering the reward for George's capture, to Mr Christmas, the governor of Knutsford Gaol, in case he went back to his birthplace.

Once notified of Howarth's possible return to the area where he had been born and had grown up, all eyes became alert to the potential. As the *Taunton Courier* reported, it is 'a singular circumstance that as Mr Gratix, a respectable solicitor of Wilmslow near Mobberley, was riding to the Chester Assizes he met a person to whom the house where George was concealed belonged and who assured him that he had seen him there that morning'. Gratix requested the man come with him to apprehend Howarth, but the criminal's reputation – despite the fact he was in no state even to resist arrest, let alone have the strength for another ferocious encounter like that with Oxley, back in Frome – was enough to make the person refuse it. 'Lord Sir! If you'd give me 500 guineas I would not venture.'

Undaunted at the prospect of coming up against George Howarth, Gratix immediately galloped back to Mobberley and 'called on the constables to aid and assist'. At first, according to the *Taunton Courier*, 'considerable hesitation was manifested here also when the nature of the business was mentioned'. Eventually, they agreed to accompany Gratix, and made their way to the house where Howarth was hiding.

On arrival, the men found the door was not fastened and George Howarth was alone in the room. As Gratix informed him that he was his prisoner, Peter Howarth (George's brother) came downstairs and, realising what was going on, attempted to grab a pitchfork, but one of the constables in attendance, perceiving his intention, sprang forward and secured the weapon before the brother could reach it.

George Howarth was then taken to Knutsford Gaol, where he was identified a few days later by Joseph Oxley, who made the trip up to Knutsford after receiving a letter from the governor informing him of the capture. Once Howarth had been identified, the substantial reward of 100 guineas was immediately paid to Mr Gratix. He, in turn, gave Oxley £10 of the reward money and presented him with an elegant snuff box 'as a compliment for his courageous conduct in apprehending such a desperate character and thereby dispersing the most extraordinary and systematic gang of thieves that ever infested any neighbourhood.'

Oxley then accompanied Howarth back to Frome on the Oxford Mail Coach, along with a Mr Lee, stopping at Bristol and Bath and finally boarding the Poole-bound coach for the final stretch to Frome. At the various stops on the way from Knutsford, huge crowds gathered to catch a glimpse of Howarth, who by now had become a famous if notorious, 'newspaper celebrity'.

The *Bath Herald*, reported that:

> *he did not by any means seem so powerful a man as had been represented, but we understand his appearance is much altered for the worse owing to the dreadful sufferings and privations he must have undergone since his escape. He was described as of 'very suspicious appearance' and very heavily ironed with an immense pair of wooden shoes which prevented every possibility of escape. The prisoner did not appear to be in the least affected by his situation nor did he once glance at the numerous crowd assembled to see him, but sat eating bread and cheese with avidity. As he approached Frome however, his spirits became subdued and tears were observed to start from his eyes. On his arrival, he was taken to the Blind House* [located in a corner of St John's Churchyard, in Frome and still extant today – if never used] *where his wife was permitted to see him and the scene was very affecting and they embraced several times.*

The guardhouse where George Howarth and many of his kind have found themselves locked up. The Blue Boar is conspicuously and conveniently next door. (Frome Museum)

Now that George was back in Frome, things didn't look too good. The day after his return, Thursday 6 September 1827, he was brought up by Mr Culverhouse the constable, to be examined by the magistrates at the Assembly Rooms above the George Inn. He was still strongly secured in irons as he faced the numerous charges, which included the cutting and maiming of Joseph Oxley, a robbery at Christ Church, and the theft of the thirteen blankets from the parish manufactory. After witnesses were called to attest to these criminal acts, the magistrates quickly reached their verdict and Howarth was fully committed to Ilchester Gaol to stand trial at the next assizes.

While languishing in Ilchester Gaol, and with his recent exploits fully known, the local papers had a field day with this new found 'celebrity' and over the coming period, various articles painted a fascinating picture of the Howarths. For example, during the sixteen-year period that the Howarth brothers had been inhabitants of Frome, sheep and calves had been stolen from fields, joints of meat from butchers' shops, cloth from factories; even sacrilege had been committed. Frequently, innocent persons (such as the man falsely accused of stealing the parish bag) had been arraigned on suspicion of committing these crimes.

What was most incredible though, according to many of the newspapers, was that throughout their criminal activities, they had maintained the respect of those who knew them to such an extraordinary degree that to have spoken a word against their good name would have been considered an insult. Ralph Howarth was a constant attendant at the Methodist Church and respected as a leader of the local Methodist Society, while George's wife was a devout member. In fact, the two brothers had attended a prayer meeting only hours before the robbery at Oxley's and a private prayer meeting was set to take place at Ralph's house on the Monday morning, had not fate and the law intervened. Paradoxically, the brothers' seemed to hold the established church in contempt, because not only did George's wife take pride in her gown made from the clergyman's surplice and Ralph's wife wear a velvet bonnet made from a pulpit cushion, but 'When the church was robbed of these articles, the sacrament wine was drunk, and an indecency committed in the flagon which had contained it!'

At the same time, they were known as being very generous, giving away joints of meat to those people less well off. The truth was, they had so much meat that when Ralph's house was raided, a secret cupboard was discovered on the stairs where part of this stolen meat was deposited. While at George's house, they found a belt with two hooks at the back and two straps which buckled around the shoulders; the means by which a strong man could carry an immense weight (it was well known that George could carry 10cwt on his shoulders, so a couple of sheep would have been easy for him).

George Howarth's trial at the assize court in Taunton took place on Tuesday 3 April 1828, in front of Mr Justice Littledale. The accused appeared dejected and stood with his arms crossed in a 'declining posture' with his head held very low. He was charged with several offences, many connected with the attack on Joseph Oxley. When asked how he pleaded, Howarth raised his head slightly and said in an almost inaudible voice, 'Not Guilty'.

According to newspaper reports, he appeared very different from the fearless, muscular brute that many expected; such was the awe inspired by his reputation that Lithographic prints of him and his former residence were exhibited in many of the stationers' shops in Taunton.

The prisoner was asked if he had anything to say and replied that he did not, but hoped for mercy. He asked the gaoler for permission to sit down; when this was refused, he burst into tears and continued weeping for a short time. The jury was asked to consider its verdict on all the charges arising from the Oxley burglary and found him guilty on most of them.

George Howarth was sentenced to be transported for a total of fourteen years – but the matter was not over yet. One of the burglary charges against him was that he had been in a garden, 'for an unlawful purpose and that then and there, in order to prevent his lawful apprehension, he maliciously cut and stabbed with intent to murder.' His defence counsel Mr Earle raised several objections to this charge on a matter of law and Justice Littledale ruled that it should be reserved for further consideration before a higher court.

The act in contention was Lord Ellenborough's Act, or the Malicious Cutting and Stabbing Act of 1803, which carried a death sentence on conviction if it could be proven that the 'cutting and stabbing' had been carried out to resist lawful arrest while in the commission of a crime. The defence point was that Howarth had moved on unobserved from the scene of the crime, was no longer committing it, and that being in someone else's garden was not a felony. In which case, Howarth was quite justified in defending himself and could not be convicted of that charge.

Howarth had to wait four months to receive the decision and unsurprisingly it went against him; Mr Justice Park ruling, at Wells, that the law had been considered by nine judges and the trial judge, and they had unanimously decided the point could not be sustained. In their opinion, the time from when Howarth was first seen in the wood store until he was captured in the garden while using the sword to wound Oxley to avoid capture, came within the meaning of the Act because he was still in contemplation of the felony. The conviction was confirmed and the law had to take its course. The learned judge did not mince his words:

> *Under these circumstances, said his Lordship, your life is forfeited to the laws of your country and from what I have ascertained of the catalogue of your offences you have certainly been a wicked and desperate character; the sentence of death must therefore be recorded against you; whether you will suffer the penalty due to your crimes depends on the recommendation to be made to his majesty. I would not have you flatter yourself that your life will be spared, but prepare yourself to meet the contrary event. If, however, the former should be the case it will be for the purposes of ridding this happy country of you for the term of your natural life.*

His Lordship then ordered the sentence of death to be recorded against the prisoner who, during the time he was at the bar, rested both his hands on the rail, bending his head down as much as possible to prevent his countenance from being seen by the numbers who thronged the court to hear his sentence. He appeared unmoved at his fate and departed from the dock without betraying the least emotion.

Despite the death sentence imposed on George Howarth, it seems the trial judge, Justice Littledale, had at some point 'humanely interposed on his behalf', presumably seeing some good in him, and so he received a reprieve and was sentenced to be transported for life. Therefore, on 8 September 1828, at the age of 58, Howarth was moved to the *Captivity* to await transportation; the very place that his brother Ralph had been sent one year before. He was there until 30 April the following year when he was sent aboard the *York* and set sail for Van Diemen's Land, now Tasmania, to serve out the remainder of his days. It is unlikely that the brothers in crime saw each other again.

Chapter 6

All Hell Broke Loose!

A fatal encounter at the Angel & Crown, 1830

The Angel and Crown public house was situated in an impressive range of buildings located at No. 39, Vallis Way, on the outskirts of Frome. When the last pint was poured in 1960, it had been quenching the thirst of the local population for more than two centuries. Until about 1770, it was known as The Angel, and was one of several properties in the area owned by Richard Treasure, but by the time it appeared on the 1774 map of Frome, it had acquired the additional 'Crown'.

It was sold in 1825 and in the *Salisbury & Wiltshire Journal* announcing its sale, described it as 'long established, convenient and roomy, with malt house, brewhouse, three cellars, two stables outbuildings, large yard and appurtenances.' The new occupier was a Charles Bishop, but he went bankrupt not long afterwards. Despite this, it continued to operate as an inn and was, by all accounts, a warm and friendly hostelry, which did little, in terms of unwarranted incidents, to draw attention to itself. This all changed one night in June 1830 when 'all hell broke loose'.

On the evening of Wednesday 2 June 1830, Benjamin Butcher, a saddler, and his millwright brother, were sitting with friends in the tap room of the Angel & Crown and enjoying a few drinks. Around 9.30 in the evening two Irish brothers – Michael and Matthew Teaken – entered the premises. They went up to the bar and began talking to a girl named Lydia Jones, who would later be described by a newspaper account as being of 'light character'. The nature of their conversation became risqué and a wager regarding Jones was made; the content of which, was deemed so indecent that before it was read out as evidence at the trial, it was ordered that 'females were not permitted to enter the court'.

The Angel & Crown as it looks today. In 1830 George Butcher was killed here. (Authors' Collection)

On overhearing this lewd conversation, Benjamin Butcher made a remark to the newcomers. Some retort was no doubt returned, as Butcher stood up, took off his hat and coat, and was ready to fight the Teaken brothers. The opening salvo was a slap across Matthew Teaken's face with his open hand, but before Butcher could do anything else, Michael Teaken grabbed a large poker from the fireplace and, grasping it tightly with both hands, struck Butcher above the right eye with such a violent blow that it instantly felled him to the ground and fractured his skull. As Butcher lay unconscious on the inn floor, his brother stepped forward but was also hit by Teaken in almost the same place on his head and knocked senseless.

As the fight spread to include the friends of the Butcher brothers, two more Irishmen entered the bar. Seeing what was happening, they turned and went back to the door, but only to ensure no one could escape. During the brawl that followed, another man, Morgan, was seriously hurt and by its end, according to one report on the incident, 'the lower part of the [public] house was completely drenched in blood'.

The quartet of Irishmen then fled the pub, taking the poker with them, although two of them didn't go very far. In a somewhat inexplicable decision, they made their way to the next pub along the road: The Ship [today known as The Artisan] at the top of Catherine Street. Here they were quickly apprehended and taken before the magistrates, the other two being arrested shortly afterwards. The foursome was described as 'duffers' or hawkers of small items, and along with Michael and Matthew Teaken, were identified as Patrick Keating and a man named McMullin.

Michael Teaken admitted that he had struck the blows and was sent to Shepton Gaol. While he was there, however, Benjamin Butcher died. He had managed to cling to life until Monday 14 June, nearly two weeks after receiving his injuries. A formal inquest was held at the George Hotel, in Frome's Market Place, two days later, before Daniel Ashford Esq, the coroner for East Somerset and a jury of twelve 'honest and true' gentlemen. The evidence given by Mr Bush the surgeon who proved that Butcher's death was caused by the blow inflicted by Michael Teaken. Within a short time, the Jury returned their verdict that the victim had met his end by 'Wilful Murder'. Benjamin Butcher left a wife and three children. His assailant was committed for trial at the next Somerset Assizes.

Michael Teaken was 21 years old at the time of the offence, an Irishman from Kilkeel, County Down in the north of Ireland. He was described as 5ft 5¼in, stout, with a long face, fresh complexion, sandy hair, light hazel eyes, and 'much freckled in the face'! His occupation was described as traveller, he was single and could read and write.

On 14 August 1830, at the Crown Court Summer Assizes, then sitting in Bridgwater before Justice Baron Vaughan, Michael Teaken was on trial supposedly for murder, but before proceedings began, the difference between murder and manslaughter was carefully explained to the jury by the prosecution, Mr Jeremy, who pointed out,

> *the necessity of their firmly awarding the penalty for the crime of murder, unless, as he hoped would be the case, any mitigating proof should be elicited to bring it down to the lesser offence of*

> *manslaughter. He explained the law observing that if from any intentionally violent means death ensued it was not necessary to prove 'malice prepense'* [i.e. intention to kill] *if there were, on the other hand no provocation proved.*

A number of witnesses were brought to give evidence which revealed the Butchers were 'fighting characters' and induced a belief that the prisoner struck out in self-defence. This was also confirmed by one of the witnesses, George Jelly, who, it was reported, 'gave his testimony with great accuracy and consistency showing that many expressions tending to excite anger were used towards the Irishmen who all appeared peaceably inclined until urged on to fight'. Jelly gave further evidence that Teaken thought himself in danger and took up the poker in self-defence. This, together with the testimony of several others who had known Teaken for some time and who spoke of his generally peaceable and inoffensive disposition, induced the jury to acquit him of murder and find him guilty of manslaughter.

Michael Teaken was sentenced to be transported to Australia for life. He entered Ilchester Gaol on 22 August 1830, but on 20 September was moved to the *Captivity* following a brief spell in Millbank Prison, London.

Milbank was a massive gaol that was said to have cost half a million pounds to build. In Peter Cunningham's *Handbook of London*, published in 1850, the author described Millbank as:

> *A mass of brickwork equal to a fortress, on the left bank of the Thames, close to Vauxhall Bridge; erected on ground bought in 1799 of the Marquis of Salisbury … The external walls form an irregular octagon, and enclose upwards of sixteen acres of land. Its ground-plan resembles a wheel, the governor's house occupying a circle in the centre, from which radiate six piles of building, terminating externally in towers. The ground on which it stands is raised but little above the river, and was at one time considered unhealthy.*

Millbank had originally been called 'The Penitentiary' or 'Penitentiary House for London and Middlesex' and was the largest prison in London. Every convict – male and female – sentenced to transportation was sent first to Millbank, to await the sentence being carried out. Here they remained for about three months under the close supervision of the prison inspectors (though Teaken was there for less than a month). At the end of this time-period the inspectors (there were normally three of them) reported to the Home Secretary, and recommended the place of transportation. According to Cunningham, '[t]he number of persons in Great Britain and Ireland condemned to transportation every year [amounted] to about 4000'.

Convicts awaiting transportation were kept in solitary confinement and in silence for the first six months of their sentence, although this 'silent' system would gradually be abolished within the next couple of decades. Mayhew and Binny, in their monumental work *The Criminal Prisons of London*, published in the late nineteenth century, described the routine that would have existed at that time, but one can assume that it was very similar to when Teaken was there:

> *On the arrival of the prisoners at Millbank, the governor informed us, they are examined by the surgeon, when, if pronounced free from contagious disease, they are placed in the reception ward, and afterwards distributed throughout the prison according to circumstances, having been previously bathed and examined, naked, as at Pentonville. 'If a prisoner be ordered to be placed in association on medical grounds,' added the governor, 'the order is entered in the book in red ink, otherwise he is located in one of the various pentagons for six months, to undergo confinement in separate cell. On entering his cell, each prisoner's hair is cut, and the rules of the prison are read over to him, the latter process being repeated every week, and the hair cut as often as required.'*

In September 1830 Teaken was transferred to the next stage of the transportation process: a prison hulk. Late in the eighteenth century, with exile to America no longer a possibility, prisons within England began to become overcrowded. Someone had the idea of using the rotting hulks of decommissioned ships as temporary storage for this surplus population, until their passage to the new colonies in Australia, or other fate, could be determined.

The hulks were intended as a 'makeshift under pressing circumstances', but continued for more than half a century, despite being condemned by all those concerned with prison administration and conditions. Most prisoners from Somerset were sent to hulks in Plymouth or Woolwich, as was Teaken, although it depended on where space was available.

On arrival, Teaken would have been bathed, de-loused, issued with a coarse uniform and placed in leg irons. The convicts would be sent ashore during the day to carry out heavy labouring work and other menial tasks, mainly stacking timber, loading and unloading vessels or scraping rust. Gone now were the 'cosy' cells and quiet atmosphere of Millbank and here were 'messes', with forty or fifty hammocks in a line, like rows of canvas boats, where the prisoners were expected to sleep every night.

In the early days of the prison hulks, those to be transported would be held on board until there was room on the next ship to Australia. Mayhew and Binny, spent more than twenty pages in *The Criminal Prisons of London* describing in detail the daily life on board a similar ship, the *Defence,* and so we can perhaps get a somewhat intimate picture of what Teaken's life during his time, on board his own hulk, would have been like.

Michael Teaken, along with all his fellow convicts, would have been woken at 5.30 a.m. They would then get dressed into their rusty-brown red-striped suits, roll up their hammocks, and have breakfast; this normally consisted of 12oz of bread and a pint of cocoa. Dinner would be 4oz of cooked meat, half a pint of soup, ½lb of potatoes and 6oz of bread, while supper was one pint of tea and 8oz of bread. After breakfast, certain prisoners were rowed ashore and formed into gangs for work. At 5.15 p.m. the convicts were returned to their 'ship' and after supper could rest until chapel at 8 p.m. They returned to their hammocks at 9 p.m. Convicts were allowed visits from relatives once every three months, or could write home after a similar period.

Teaken stayed on board the *Captivity* until March 1831, when he boarded *The Argyle*, to be taken to Van Diemen's Land, now known as Tasmania. The next we hear of him is a decade later, in October 1841, when he is recorded as being in the police office at Brighton, a district of the prison island.

By 1847, he is living in Hobart Town, still on the island, but has now received permission to marry according to the rites and ceremonies of the Church of Scotland. His bride, one Alice Fitzgerald, is simply described as a spinster aged over 21. They have a son, John, in 1849, and it seems Teaken has settled down and is making the best of his new life in Australia, having served his time for a moment of impassioned violence nearly twenty years beforehand.

Had his friends in Frome not spoken up for him all those years ago, the tale might have had a very different outcome.

Chapter 7

I Predict a Riot

Thomas Champneys and the Frome Election, 1832

It is said that there are three sides to every story – yours, mine and the truth! This certainly seems to be the case with an incident that occurred in 1832 – one that left death, destruction and deceit in its wake and all in the name of politics. The incident was rioting, which accompanied the elections for the first Member of Parliament for Frome. Although there are certain universally accepted facts surrounding the rioting, including the outcome, what went on during the three days of polling is up for debate and depends on whose version you believe.

Sweeping change came to Frome in the early 1830s, mainly through the Great Reform Act of 1832. Up until that point, the town had no official representation in the Houses of Parliament, despite a population of 12,240 (according to the 1831 census), while somewhere like Old Sarum, across the county border in Wiltshire, had only three houses and seven eligible voters, but two seats. The latter was known as a rotten borough; seats that could either be easily bought or else whose result was usually decided by the main landowner within it. Before 1832, those gentlemen and landed gentry in Frome and the immediate vicinity who wanted to have their voice heard in parliament had to go to Wells to cast their vote and even then, it was as part of the county of Somerset.

All this changed then, in 1832, when parliamentary elections were to be held for the first time in the new borough of Frome, with polling to take place between tenth and twelfth of December that year at the George Inn in the town centre. At the same time, many small landowners, tenant farmers and local shopkeepers could vote for the first time and in Frome the total electorate was increased to slightly more than 300.

Despite being in his mid-60s, Sir Thomas Champneys, the master of nearby Orchardleigh, renowned bankrupt and subject of much gossip and scandal about the town, decided to stand as the Tory candidate. His opponent, Thomas Sheppard, the woollen-mill owner and local businessman, stood for the Whigs. The Champneys and Sheppard families were already sworn enemies, having been so since a bitter dispute over the command of local infantry companies almost thirty years earlier, and the forthcoming election would inflame their animosity even further.

As well as being three sides to every story, it is also often said that history is written by the winners, and this seems to have been certainly true of the events of December 1832. The normally accepted view of what happened was the subject of a long report entitled 'The Narrative of the Frome Riot' issued by Thomas Sheppard and his supporters. The following is a summary of their version of events:

On Monday 10 December, about forty of Mr Sheppard's supporters arrived at Cork Street at 9 a.m., 'without weapons of any sort' and waited patiently for the speeches to begin. Sir Thomas Champneys and his 'many hundreds' of supporters arrived at about 10.30, both on foot and mounted, but all armed in some way and seemingly ready for trouble. They immediately drove Sheppard's men away from the hustings at the George and occupied the area.

Thomas Sheppard then arrived, attended by 'at least one third of the constituency' and about 600 men from his factories. A Tory supporter attacked Sheppard as he was getting out of his carriage 'tearing the coat from his back', and this gave rise to a general free for all, which was eventually calmed down enough for speeches to be made. These were to be made from the balcony of the George.

Champneys spoke first at great length and was loudly cheered by his supporters, with their cry of 'Champneys Forever', but beneath the balcony followers of Mr Sheppard were suffering violent and unprovoked attacks. By 6.00 p.m. that day, Mr Thomas Ford of Short Street near Chapmanslade, a weaver and possibly a friend of Mr Sheppard, had been so badly beaten by the mob that he died of a 'bursting of the small intestine' on the following Thursday.

As soon as Thomas Sheppard stood to speak, the noise was so great with jeering, insults and stones being thrown that he could not be heard. According to the report, the Tory supporters

NARRATIVE
OF
FROME RIOT,
December, 1832.

We, the undersigned, declare that we have investigated the Facts stated in the following Narrative, and that we believe it to be true.

The Nomination of Candidates for Representing the new Borough of Frome was holden on Monday the 10th. of December instant.

About nine o'clock in the Morning about forty men on foot, bearing Mr. Sheppard's Favors, and without Weapons of any sort, came to Cork Street; and stood quietly near, but not on the Steps of the Hustings, to protect the approach to them.

Sir Thomas S. M. Champneys, Bart. arrived at Half-past Ten, accompanied by many hundred Men and Boys, many of them armed with Bludgeons and Cudgels: most of them were on foot, but they were attended by Men on horseback. A great number of them wore *White Ribbons*, White Sashes, or Cards inscribed with Sir Thomas Champneys' name; many of them appeared not to be Men of Frome; some of their Bludgeons and Cudgels were loaded with lead.

Some of this Party immediately assailed Mr. T. Sheppard's Men, and drove them away from the Hustings. The Men wearing White Colours, then took possession of the ground round the Hustings, and of the Upper Market Place, in front.

Soon after, Mr. Thomas Sheppard, attended by a very considerable number (perhaps about five hundred) of supporters, none of them with Sticks or Weapons of any sort, entered the *Lower* Market Place. [We have enquired most particularly, and we find that a request was made by Messrs. Sheppard that not one Weapon or Stick should be carried by the persons in their procession.] A large party of Men, both foot and horse, wearing White Colours, then moved from the Hustings to meet them; and those who preceded Mr. Sheppard's Carriage were stopped, and driven back by this Party, who formed across the road; and Mr. Thomas Sheppard's Men being driven to the left, and the contest being on that side, Mr. Thomas Sheppard's Postillions took advantage of that circumstance, and drove on the right up to the Hustings. Mr. Thomas Sheppard and his Friends near him were then assaulted by some of the other party, who opposed his entrance to the Hustings, and tore part of his and some of his Friends' Coats from off their Backs.

With great difficulty Mr. T. Sheppard and several of his Friends ascended the Hustings, and the business proceeded.

Mr. Dunn, of Frome, nominated Mr. T. Sheppard, and was seconded by Mr. John Sinkins. Mr. Hawkes, of Frome, nominated Sir Thomas Champneys, and was seconded by Mr. Jonathan Drew.

On Mr. Thomas Sheppard's attempting to speak to the Meeting, his voice was drowned by clamour; and, during the whole day, he was unable to obtain a hearing; stones and other missiles were also thrown at him.

Sir Thomas Champneys then addressed the Assembly at great length, and was loudly cheered by his party, and not interrupted by Mr. Thomas Sheppard or his Party

Violent and unprovoked attacks were made beneath the Hustings, and in other places, on the Friends of Mr. Thomas Sheppard, several times during the Morning.

One poor inoffensive Man, Thomas Ford, who offered no provocation, and whose only crime was that he was a Friend to Mr. Sheppard, was used so brutally that he died on the Thursday following. And so much violence was shewn by the riotous party, that a Requisition was made to the Magistrates to swear in Special Constables, to preserve the peace of the Town.

Captain Edgell, R.N. of Standerwick-Court, and the Reverend George Rous, Rector of Laverton, Magistrates of the Division of Frome, commenced swearing in Special Constables, at the George Inn, at Six o'clock in the Evening.

Shortly after, a numerous and formidable Mob of Men with White Colours, many of whom were recognized as the Men who attended Sir Thomas Champneys, on his Entry, armed with Cudgels, Bludgeons, and Stones, without having *received any provocation* by the Magistrates or Special Constables, forced their way into the George Inn and made an attack on the Magistrates and Constables.

After a very severe conflict, which continued more than an hour, and in which several on both sides were very seriously wounded, and the Inn much damaged, the assailants were driven out, and the Door strongly barricaded: but the Threats, as well as the Conduct of the Rioters were so formidable, that the Magistrates sent for a Troop of the Seventh Regiment of Dragoons, stationed at Trowbridge, who arrived most promptly that Night.

In the mean while the Inn was beset by the Mob, who deliberately broke the Windows, and excluded any public communication with the Persons within.

During this and the following days an attack on Mr. George Sheppard's House being apprehended, three hundred Men were kept by Mr. G. Sheppard at his House, at Frome-Field; and also about two hundred Men divided between Mr. Byard Sheppard's and Mr. William Sheppard's Houses, and at their different Factories,—these Men, after Monday Morning, never going to the Market-Place, or interfering with what was going on there, or in any degree with the Election, otherwise than guarding these Buildings, except about fifty who were sworn in Special Constables.

The next Morning (Tuesday) the Military marched out of Town to Beckington, with orders to remain there during the Polling, and to return when the Poll was closed.—The Men were Mounted and about to move off, when Sir Thomas Champneys arrived.

The Polling was adjourned for an hour, that the Military might be quite removed before it began.

The Polling then commenced, and Sir Thomas Champneys' Voters went to the Polling-Room, from Cork-Street, through the Market-House, which the Room adjoined; and Mr. Thomas Sheppard's Voters went, at first, through the George Inn front door, but about Eleven o'clock being interrupted from going that way, went by a Private Way through the Crown Inn, and a sort of Cellar of the George.

About noon, an attempt was made by the Mob to force an entrance into the George Inn, which was resolutely resisted by the Special Constables; several of them suffered from the Bludgeons and Stones of the Assailants. The George Inn front Door was now again barricaded.

Many more of the Inhabitants of Frome were sworn in as Special Constables during this Morning.

Mr. T. Sheppard did not appear on this day at the Hustings or in the Town, as his Friends and the Magistrates wished to prevent any cause of additional excitement in the Mob.

On this as well as on the preceding day, many of Mr. Thomas Sheppard's Supporters were, without provocation, attacked and ill treated by the Bludgeon Men wearing White Colors, and in the Evening the Windows of several others of Mr. Thomas Sheppard's Supporters were demolished, and some of their Houses much injured externally and internally.

A little more than an hour after the Polling was over, the *Dragoons* again entered the Town, and remained until about half an hour before the Polling commenced on the next day.

Before the Polling commenced on Wednesday, Captain Edgell, one of the Magistrates, stated on the Hustings to Sir Thomas Champneys, that some of the Special Constables were armed with *Fire-Arms*, and that, if such Violence took place as on the preceding days, they would be ordered by the Magistrates to Fire.

On the Wednesday, Mr. T. Sheppard, at the request of the Magistrates and his *Friends*, again abstained from appearing in the Town. By about ten o'clock, on this day, Mr. Thomas Sheppard had Polled 163 Votes, which were more than half of the whole number of Persons having Votes; so that Sir Thomas Champneys, even if he should have Polled every other Voter, could not have been returned. Indeed the original number on the *List of Voters* being 322, and many having, since the *List* was Printed and before the Election, been struck off from change of Residence and other causes; the number of 163 was considerably above half. At about Eleven o'clock, the Mob commenced deliberately pelting at the *remaining* Windows of the George Inn; and continued doing so for an hour or two.

Between one and two o'clock P. M. a large body of the Mob wearing White Ribbons and Favours, (many of whom were recognized as the same Men who attended Sir Thomas Champneys' entry,) and shouting, 'Champney for ever,' made a most furious attack on the Crown Inn, (through which, and the George Inn, Mr. Sheppard's Voters passed to the place where the Poll was taken,) for the purpose, it is supposed, *of forcing* their way into the George Inn, which having been barricaded since the attack on the preceding day, could only be approached this way.

The Mob effected an entrance; and proceeded to demolish the Bar: one of the Special Constables had his arm broken, and others were most seriously injured, in attempting to oppose them. The Magistrates then ordered the Special Constables, about twelve of whom were armed with Carbines, to make a sally from the George through the Crown and repel the assailants. They succeeded in driving them from the Crown, and in clearing the space in front of that Inn, and of the George as far as the Hustings. The Magistrates read the Riot Act, and were both struck with stones; and seeing that the Mob closed again upon the Special Constables as they returned, and continued to assail them most violently with stones and brick-bats (some of which were thrown from the Hustings,) and that many were already seriously wounded, ordered them to fire. The Special Constables, many of whom were bleeding profusely from the wounds received from the Missiles, determined to preserve coolness and self-forbearance, still remained patient under the showers of Missiles which were striking them. They retreated to the Crown door, where they were again attacked by the Mob in the same manner. At length, after repeated warnings to the Mob of the consequences of their conduct, and earnest entreaties that they would *disperse*, three or four shots were fired. By these shots two men were severely wounded, one of them below the knee, whose leg it was found necessary to amputate, and the other in the thigh. These two men had taken an active part in the Riots: we are happy to find that they are both likely to recover.

The Troop of the Seventh Dragoons, who on the previous day had marched to Beckington, were recalled, and entered the Town about Three o'clock, which necessarily stopped the Poll.

Shortly after the firing, Sir Thomas Champneys went home, and in the Evening sent in his Resignation to the Returning Officer, requiring that the Poll should be opened *pro forma* on the following Morning, giving Notice that such Resignation was without prejudice to any proceedings he might institute as to the Election being illegal.

The Poll was opened on the Thursday, but no Votes were tendered; and at the Close of the Poll the Numbers were as follow:—

Mr. T. SHEPPARD....163
Sir T. CHAMPNEYS ..100

Majority for Mr. SHEPPARD....63

This Narrative must not be concluded without congratulating all the respectable portion of the Inhabitants of Frome, on possessing in their Neighbourhood two such Magistrates as Captain Edgell and the Rev. Mr. Rous, who, during the whole of these three most disgraceful Days, shewed unremitting attention to the Duties of their Station.

It should be also mentioned respecting the two other Magistrates of this Division, that one of them, the Earl of Cork, was in Ireland, and the other, the Rev. Mr. Sainsbury, of Beckington, confined by Illness.

The Rev. F. Doveton, of Mells, a Magistrate of the Division of Mells and Leigh, came to Frome and assisted on Wednesday, and remained until Friday.

To the judicious arrangements of these worthy Magistrates, and to the manner in which they were carried into effect, the Borough of Frome owes its escape from a Devastation similar to that of Bristol.—And, by these Measures, even the infuriated Mob were saved from the Carnage which must have ensued, if it had become necessary to prevent their Outrages by Means of the Military.

Frome, 22nd. December, 1832.

J. A Wickham,	James Baller,	William Giles,	Daniel Bennett,
Thomas Bunn,	Geo. Messiter	Edmund D. Wickham,	Richard Major,
G. M. George,	Daniel Trotman,	Samuel Porter,	W. P. Penny,
J. C. Yeatman,	Harry Hams,	Edward Cockey,	James Holliday,
F. Allen,	Alfred Harrold,	George Allen,	Thomas West,
James Edwards,	Joseph Hopkins,	James Kenwood,	George H. Means,
John Harrold,	Samuel Trotman,	William Hams,	Christopher Moreby,
Henry Brittain,	Samuel Gregory,	Henry Nicholls,	Richard Strong,
George Walters,	Thomas Charles,	James Hill,	L. Perman,
J. W. Little,	John Bridgman,	William Brown,	Samuel Hodder,
W. Nias,	Thomas Pitt,	Thomas Scudamore	J. Plaister,
J. Dommett,	E. G. Pitt,	William Harrold,	R. Deacon,
John Sinkins,	Henry Hillier, Jun.	J. V. Buckler,	Henry Dudden,
Charles Oldfield,	H. Crum,	Thomas Cruse,	John Hannings,
John Rossiter,	Jacob Player,	John Nicholls, jun.	J. Gregory,
William Cockey,	Lewis Coward,	John Guyer,	Robert Hiscocks,
Henry Rotton,	Barlow Slade,	Elisha King,	John Olive,
W. Rossiter,	J. W. D. Wickham,	G. S. Ward,	Francis Bush,
Edmund Gregory,	W. M. H. Williams,	T. R. Ward,	Francis John Bush.

PENNY, PRINTER AND BOOKSELLER, FROME.

Narrative of Frome Riot. *An early case of spin?* (Frome Museum) 'attacked every person who wore the colours of Mr Sheppard, tore down his banners & broke the poles into bludgeons'.

Things had got so out of hand that special constables were being sworn in and while this was going on a 'numerous & formidable mob' (belonging to Champneys' camp) forced their way into the George and attacked the magistrates and constables. The conflict continued for over an hour during which men on both sides were seriously injured and the inn much damaged before the assailants were driven out and the door barricaded. No polling took place that day.

At this point the magistrates naturally started to panic and summoned a troop of dragoons from Trowbridge, who arrived most promptly. Things remained highly volatile though and 300 men were kept by Mr Sheppard to protect his house at Fromefield, to the north of the town centre, while yet more guarded his cloth manufacturing factories over the next few days.

The balcony of the George Hotel was where the two candidates aspiring to become Frome's first Member of Parliament gave their speeches in front of hostile crowds.

On Tuesday morning, the second day, the troop of soldiers were marched off to Beckington, with instructions to remain out of sight but on standby as polling began. Sir Thomas Champneys voters entered the polling room via Cork Street and the Market House, while those of Mr Sheppard should have gone through the front door of the George, but were prevented from doing so by the mob and had to enter via a cellar in the adjoining Crown. At about noon the mob again tried to force its way into the George and were resisted by the special constables who barricaded the door once more. Mr Sheppard avoided the town all day in case he inflamed the mob still further and once the polling was over the dragoons were recalled and again stayed the night.

On Wednesday morning, the supposed last day of polling, Captain Edgell of the dragoons informed Sir Thomas that some of the special constables were armed and should violence break out again they would be ordered to fire. Following advice, Mr Sheppard again stayed away, but by about 10 o'clock in the morning he had polled 163 votes out of the 322 eligible voters, and it was obvious he had won (in the end only 263 votes were cast, giving Champneys a total of 100). By 11 o'clock the mob had smashed the remaining windows at the George, once more shouting their rallying cry of 'Champneys For Ever!!'

By mid-afternoon the mob had increased in number and launched a furious attack on The Crown Inn, attempting to get through to the George next door, which was still barricaded. They managed to get in and proceeded to demolish the bar; one of the special constables had his arm broken and others were seriously injured. The magistrates then ordered the special constables, about twelve of whom were armed with carbines, to make a charge from the George through the Crown to repel the assailants, which they succeeded in doing. The magistrates read the Riot Act and were met with a hail of stones and further attacks upon the constables.

At length, after repeated warnings and orders for the rioters to disperse, they had had enough and ordered those armed with carbines to open fire. Three or four shots were fired and one man lost a leg after being shot below the knee, while another had a ball enter his thigh; the rioters turned and ran. In the end two people were killed, one being Thomas Ford who was attacked on his way home and the other being one of the rioters.

As no polling had been able to take place on the Monday, the polls re-opened on the Thursday morning but there were no more votes and to his apparent astonishment, Champneys had lost the election to Sheppard by a majority of 63 votes. The dragoons were recalled for the night once more and Sir Thomas left to return to Orchardleigh with a large party of followers.

Despite the two fatalities, it seemed that the affair was not without its humorous side. In a letter to the *Somerset Standard* in 1925, following an article on the events, a man recalled his father telling the following story:

> *The rival candidates were standing on the balcony of the George to deliver their addresses. Mr Sheppard was not a fluent speaker and had his speech written out and placed in his hat, which he held in front of him and read off his speech from it. Sir Thomas Champneys saw what was going on and called out to the crowd, 'Gentlemen you must not let your honourable candidate stand bear headed in this inclement weather – beg him to put on his hat' The people shouted, 'Put on your hat!' and when this was done the flow of eloquence was dammed at the source.*

On Saturday 29 December 1832, Sir Thomas Champneys issued a statement from his home at Orchardleigh, having just read his rival's account of events, which he described as 'a tissue of concocted falsehoods and low bred autobiography'. He does not have a lot to say but takes issue with a couple of points. The men accompanying him on the day of nomination consisted of his tenants, neighbouring yeomanry and burgesses of Frome who had, 'unsolicited, paid me the compliment to breakfast at Orchardleigh'.

Champneys then numbers his attendant supporters as 'at least 5,000 who congregated in the most orderly and joyous manner' and states that once the trouble started he spoke to Captain Edgell and they agreed to appeal to the crowd for calm and for them to 'refrain from any outrage' (Edgell also stated that 'as for breaking windows, we must always expect that in a contested election'). Sir Thomas also stated that he asked those carrying sticks and staves to give them up and that they agreed instantly to this, only to be then attacked by infuriated 'constables' who commenced hostilities.

Although Sir Thomas admitted that stones had been thrown from the George, it was only by 'skulking villains' among those already inside and he goes on to say that he was,

> *deliberately levelled at by two ruffians from below with loaded muskets one of which flashed in the pan and was again re-cocked and re-presented and from the musket of the other which was fired in a more elevated position, I now possess the bullet, which was flattened by the wall against which it struck.*

Champneys also claims that Mr Ford, the man who was attacked and died on his way home, was not a friend or supporter of Mr Sheppard as had been claimed, but merely someone who had worked at their clothing factory more than two and a half years beforehand. He finishes his short note with the following flourishes:

> *Been put forth to form a shield, as many of the names attached to it* [The Narrative] *vainly imagine, to their wanton blood thirsty operations on Wednesday, which drove me from a position where with one pointed finger and three words of exhortation, (even hoarse and exhausted as I was) enabled me to lead 10,000 persons to the confines of the town where I took my leave but at parting formed a resolution that I never would again expose myself to the comments of ungrateful, mischief-minded men by showing that forbearance which emanated from my heart and has been so completely thrown away upon the set who have signed this narrative.*

'The Narrative of the Frome Riot' was signed by almost eighty people, who declared that 'we have investigated the facts stated in the following narrative and we believe it to be true'. Near the top of the list was the name of George Messiter, a local solicitor who had been prosecuted years before for spreading rumours of Champneys being involved in homosexual practices about the town. His name was followed by at least eight people from the church vestry list who had sided with Reverend Ireland in the great sexton debate twenty-four years earlier, along with many other family names that match. Doubtless there would have been more had not the intervening twenty-four years taken its toll.

Is this evidence of a feud going back decades, if not generations? Was the anti-Champneys camp made up of those to whom the family had long owed money? Sadly, there is not enough surviving evidence to provide an answer but there is a lot more to this story than would appear at first glance.

It seems there really are two sides to every story and then there's the truth, although possibly to get a little nearer to the latter, we need only look to the following spring, when the trial of those arrested during the election riots opened. On 3 March 1833, James Wheeler, Richard Hill, Joseph Stokes, Henry Gregory, Joseph Short & Samuel Button were charged with riotous assembly and assaulting two constables in the execution of their duty. Charges against four other men of 'maliciously shouting' were dropped.

Local magistrate and rector of Laverton the Reverend George Rous was the first prosecution witness and he set the scene. Rous explained that by the Tuesday morning about 200 special constables had been selected and were subject to a hail of stones, with many badly injured; among those involved with the swearing-in was solicitor George Messiter who, the witness agreed, 'is not friendly with Sir Thomas Champneys'. Twelve of the constables had been armed with carbines and formed a line outside the George. The Riot Act was read from the porch of the pub, but the stones kept coming and, despite repeated warnings, the mob would not disperse so the order was given to fire, which four or five of the constables did, but only once each. They were instructed to aim low and pick out the most active. Two persons were shot and as a result, one needed to have his leg amputated, and the other was still in hospital at the time of the trial.

The prisoners had been in custody since the Thursday following the election, because bail had been refused. During cross examination the defence counsel tried to imply that the constables were all Sheppard's supporters, but Rous stated that he did not know this to be the case and that line of questioning was stopped by the judge.

One of the next witnesses called was William Giles, a special constable. He testified that he saw Richard Hill and Joseph Stokes at the head of the mob threaten the constables with sticks; and that he was 'severely wounded in the face with a stone'. Henry Gregory was also there with a white ribbon, Giles continued, although without any stick. 'The mob could not attack us directly because of our bayonets. Reverend Rous said, 'Gentlemen you must fire! Four shots were fired. I did not fire.' One unnamed constable later claimed that so few shots were fired because some of the men's carbines were too damaged by the stones to fire properly. 'After the shooting, Sir Thomas's carriage was ordered and he went off most of the mob accompanying him. I voted for Mr Sheppard.'

Joseph Oxley a cooper and maltster, and the man who had brought the infamous Howarth brothers reign of crime to an end, six years earlier, was next into the witness stand. He attested that he saw Gregory daring the constables to fire at him, and said that his windows and doors were broken and his family were driven out of their house by the mob.

A host of other witnesses also gave their evidence, before the prosecution's case ended. The defence case was very short and consisted of a few witnesses stating that they had seen Gregory stop people from removing sticks from his yard and that his wife had had a lock put on the door. The defence counsel did make the point that the first magistrate to be called for the swearing in of the constables 'entered the inn of the Sheppard party' and contended that, 'if constables had been called in on both sides there would have been no riot'.

Despite strong evidence of bias, the jury convicted all the defendants, who were sentenced to eight months hard labour, with Henry Gregory bound over in his own recognisance for the sum of £50 to keep the peace for two years.

And so, the matter seemingly ended. Tribal loyalties were obviously very deep and of long standing among the populous, with the political policies of the parties not mentioned and perhaps not even relevant.

Sir Thomas Champneys died on 21 November 1839, having been declared bankrupt again in 1835, and certainly received a bad press during and after his lifetime; how much of it was deserved or down to prejudice and rivalry we don't know, but a good case can be made out for history having misjudged him. He certainly inherited the family trait of being reckless with money, which being born into enormous debt did nothing to quell, but despite having many enemies who were more than ready to spread, or maybe even create, stories about his sexual preferences, he does not seem to have had the reputation for drinking or gambling which was attached to the lost fortunes of so many of his class. Despite his financial difficulties (it was said he died owing £100,000), he nevertheless left directions for a sumptuous funeral.

As to the successful candidate of the 1832 election, Thomas Sheppard, he remained Frome's Member of Parliament until 1847. This parliamentary 'career' however, included a defection to the Conservative party in the mid-1830s and one election victory where he retained his seat by a majority of only four votes, which reputedly cost him £10,000 in bribes to achieve.

Lady Charlotte Champneys, Sir Thomas's wife, died 1845, was much respected for having paid off a great number of the family debts amounting to about £30,000. There were no children so the baronetcy and the family line ended with her, but the name lives on as a large shopping development in Llandudno – 'Mostyn Champneys Retail Parks'. There would appear to be no portraits of Sir Thomas apart from a very early one with his sister, and one of his mother by Sir Joshua Reynolds. Any personal mementoes or family papers seem to have been dispersed or lost with even the house itself demolished.

Orchardleigh Park and House became the property of Richard Henry Cox, receiver in bankruptcy who put it all up for auction in 1855, an auction that had been planned since 1849. The estate was bought by William Duckworth who tore down the ancient house and built a new one in a rather awkward jumble of styles that was fashionable at the time. The estate remained in that family until the 1980s when it was sold once more and is now a fashionable wedding venue and golf course.

CHAPTER 8

A Matter of Forgery

The manslaughter of Ferdinand Candy, 1844

On Tuesday 16 January 1844, a group of friends were drinking at a Frome public house. Sometime during the alcohol-fuelled evening an argument broke out between two of them and this led to a bare-knuckle fight in a nearby field. So brutal was the conflict that ensued, that one fighter was fatally injured, while the other, along with two spectators, ended up in gaol.

Francis Butler Daniell was a talented 23-year-old from a respectable local family who lived at Pleasant Row, Culverhill, on the southern outskirts of Frome. He lived with his 60-year-old father, Thomas, a professor of music, his mother Mary, and brothers Thomas, Henry, Edmund and Alfred. Francis had inherited his father's interest and talent for music and earned his living as an organist.

Also in the party of drinkers was another local man, Ferdinand Candy, who was 20 years of age and was the son of Thomas and Hannah Candy. He had been born in Mells, but the family now lived at Marston Bigot. Contemporary reports are sketchy, but it appears an argument broke out between the very drunk Daniell and Candy, and the latter invited the other to step outside to settle their differences. Reluctant at first, Daniell eventually consented to his companion's challenge and the pair adjourned to a nearby field. As was normal practice, they were accompanied by two seconds, a William Sargeant, a 37-year-old married labourer from Blatchbridge, and Stephen Wheeler, a 24-year-old single man who also worked as a labourer, but was described in one later account of the incident as an 'old offender'. Both men were almost 6ft in height and so, as would later become a key element in the subsequent trial, could have stopped the fight at any time had they wanted to.

Bare-knuckle fighting was a popular sport, but also a popular way of settling your differences, although sometimes it proved fatal as Ferdinand Candy found out in 1844.

The punishing contest lasted for an hour and it was reported that Candy was struck violently to the ground during each bout, until he could no longer stand and so the fight ended. A betting man would probably have favoured a farmer's boy over a musician, but Daniell was 5ft 10in in height and Candy was the more inebriated of the two. The loser, Candy, was carried to a barn and left alone to sleep it off among the straw, while Daniell, who was also severely beaten, was led away from the field of battle by the rest of the group.

The next morning Candy managed to get back to his family home in Marston – some reports say he made his own way, others, that he was retrieved by his friends and carried there. Shortly after arriving home, however, and having received no medical attention he died from the effects of the beating. It had probably been assumed, that when he was left alone in the barn, he would merely 'sleep it off' but, like John Crees nearly twenty-years earlier, nobody realised just how badly he was hurt.

Newspapers at the time hinted at 'various reports of foul play' being in circulation, 'but we refrain from giving them as the parties are in custody and an inquest is now pending before D. Ashcroft Esq. at Marston Inn.' Details of the inquest do not seem to have been reported except to say that the jury brought in a verdict of 'manslaughter'.

Francis Daniell and the two 'seconds' were arrested and charged with manslaughter and remanded to Shepton Gaol to await trial. They were confined for nearly three months awaiting the Lent Assize which opened at Taunton on 30 March 1844, before Mr Justice Whightman. After the judge summed up, the jury found all three guilty of manslaughter and he proceeded to sentence. A contemporary account reports his remarks, which are interesting regarding to whom he apportions the higher level of blame:

> *In passing sentence the learned judge remarked that the prisoners had been nearly three months already in prison, which he should take into consideration in the punishment to be inflicted. He considered the seconds more guilty than the principle as they were bound to have stopped the fight when they found how severely the deceased and the prisoner Daniell were punished. His lordship then sentenced Daniell to ten days and the other two to a fortnight's imprisonment with hard labour, the last two days in each case to be passed in solitary confinement.*

There the account might well have ended, a typical example of two 'fired up' lads having a drunken argument in a pub, which got out of hand and ended in misery for all concerned. But one question tantalisingly remains to be answered. What were they arguing about that called for so much violence? Nothing was reported in the press at the time regarding a motive for the fight, but it seems Candy was most insistent they sort their 'differences' out man to man; what could Daniell have said that upset him so?

For a possible answer, we need to go back almost five years to 1839 and a case of fraud. The Candy family were yeoman farmers living at Marston Bigot. On 22 January 1839, the eldest son Thomas, wanting to mortgage some land, visited Mr Whittington, a solicitor in nearby Bath. He told the solicitor that his father had died in 1835 and that he and the family wished to raise some money. Mr Whittington came out to the farm, viewed the land and collected some deeds from the Candy family, consisting at the time of Thomas's mother, Hannah,

Thomas himself, and younger brothers, Theophilus, William and Ferdinand. With everything seemingly in order, £490 was handed over to the family by Edward Gibbons, a Frome money lender.

Then the plan started to go wrong. It seems Thomas got greedy and went back to Whittington asking to borrow further monies. This was against a field he claimed an uncle named Selby had given him. Once more, he produced deeds and paperwork to back this up. Whittington thought he had better see the land himself and make sure that all was in order. He rode over and met a Mr Butt who was responsible for collecting local land taxes. During his enquiries, the Bath solicitor was astonished to learn that not only was there no one by the name of Selby who lived, or owned land, in the area, but that Thomas Candy's father, also Thomas, was very much alive and well and, having split from his wife, was living a few miles away with a sister!

The outcome of these revelations was that the five family members, including Ferdinand, who would have been about 18 at the time, were arrested and charged with forgery. Although it was determined that Ferdinand, the youngest son, was not involved, he was shown the forged documents and declared them to be in the handwriting of a man called James Sealy, a lawyer's clerk and, as it turned out, a brilliant forger.

When the family was put on trial, Thomas was convicted of being the instigator of the scheme and sentenced to be transported for fifteen years. Mother Hannah and son William were convicted of lesser offences and were imprisoned for two years each. The others were acquitted. Could it have been that Daniell was winding Candy up about the fate of his family which caused so much drunken fury and ultimately the loss of his life?

But what of the 'victor' of the fight and the 'seconds' who attended it? Francis Butler Daniell served his time and presumably continued with his organ playing and musical studies, but in April of 1847 he was in trouble once more. It seems that he took a watch and watch-guard from his younger brother Henry who had placed it in a tea caddy the previous evening and realised it was missing in the morning. It seems that Henry went to the police rather than confront his brother and when questioned, Francis claimed that Henry had given it to him.

Francis Daniell had left the watch with the landlord of The Crown public house in Keyford as security for payment of his bar bill. As payment was not forthcoming, the watch was redeemed by a witness named Maggs; he and Daniell went together to Wells where they sold it for 10 shillings. Daniell was arrested on a charge of stealing the watch but managed to escape. When recaptured he was tried and given three months hard labour (If the Maggs mentioned here is *the* William Maggs, one of Frome's most notorious criminals and was one of those accused of the Sarah Watts murder seven years later, Daniell was keeping very bad company indeed!)

Drink seems to have been at the heart of the young man's problems but he managed to survive. In the census of 1851 he is recorded as a professor of music, and later as father of two children by a Martha Harvey, whom he married in 1860. In the 1861 census he is shown as a violin performer living at 10 Thorne's Square, Frome. He died on 17 December 1863 at the age of 42.

As to the two 'seconds' – Stephen Wheeler and William Sargeant – the most interesting of them is the latter. According to the 1841 census, Sargeant was aged 35 and living at Blatchbridge with wife Maria, 33, and son Thomas, 15. In the description book at Wilton gaol, three years later, on his arrest over the Daniell and Candy fight, he is described as aged 38, married, 5ft 11½in, with a sallow complexion, hazel eyes, brown hair, and scars over his right eye and on his upper lip.

Giving credence to the possibility that the Maggs involved in the later 'watch' episode with Daniell *is* the notorious criminal, is the fact that he was living literally next door to Sargeant in 1841 and there remained a strong connection between them from then on.

Sargeant was again convicted in March 1850, along with the labourer George Browning, for assaulting 'several constables' while attempting to rescue a Robert Hurd from arrest, at the Unicorn Inn, in Frome. Hurd is another name that looms large in the town's criminal history. Also known as 'Frome Bob', he was a prizefighter and had served as a mercenary during the First Carlist War, in Spain. Along with Sargeant and Maggs (and William Sparrow), Hurd was arrested in 1851 as a suspect in the brutal rape and murder of a 14-year-old girl called Sarah Watts, who was killed at the isolated farm at West Woodlands, on the outskirts of Frome, where she lived with her parents (although they were at Frome market that day). During the preliminary hearing at the magistrates' court, Sargeant, who had been arrested at The Blue Boar by London detective Henry Smith, was acquitted. The other three, however, stood trial for the crime at the Taunton Assizes in April 1852.

For the assault charge back in March 1850, Sargeant and Browning were both given eighteen months in Shepton Mallet Gaol. Sargeant was released in June 1851 and so was therefore in the gaol at the time of the 1851 census, aged 46. He was described in the prison census as an 'edge tool maker', which was quite a skilled job. Nothing else is known about him, other than he was living at Butts Square at the time of his arrest over the Sarah Watts case.

Chapter 9

Thee Dost Not Know

The murder of Thomas George at Nunney, 1850

One Saturday evening in July 1861 an argument broke out between two men drinking in the Red Lion pub in The Butts, Frome, which resulted in the arrest of Henry Hillier for using threatening language towards William Davis. The court was told Davis was in the pub drinking with a neighbour when Hillier walked in. Davis recognised him and proposed a sarcastic toast, part of which was 'Any man who has ever done a foul deed, may he be found out before he dies.' As they left the pub an argument developed, with Hillier using 'very disgusting language' to describe Davis as a robber and a thief. In reply, Davis admitted using the words, 'If thee didst kill a man at Nunney, I hope thee wilt never kill me', to which Hillier replied, 'Take care, for thee dost not know'.

The magistrates took the defendant's side, commenting that although it was well known that Hillier had been suspected of the Nunney murder, more than a decade before, he had been tried and acquitted and should therefore be considered innocent and, as the complainant had been very aggravating, they dismissed the case. The event that had sparked this altercation happened eleven years before in the little village of Nunney, four miles southwest of Frome.

In the early hours of Thursday 4 April 1850, Joseph George discovered the body of his 17-year-old son Thomas lying in a barn with his throat cut. The George family lived in Nunney on the corner of Russell's Barton and the Market Place and worked as farm labourers for Sidney and Simon Hoddinott. The Hoddinotts owned Manor Farm, adjacent to the famous Nunney Castle. The day before, father and son had left work at about 6.30 p.m. and gone home. Joseph went straight to bed, but Thomas washed, changed clothes and went back out for the

Nunney Market Place, 2016. Russell's Barton is the small opening to the right. (Authors' Collection)

evening at about 7 o'clock. His mother, Mary, sat up waiting for him until after midnight, before going to bed herself but, unable to sleep, she became alarmed when there was still no sign of Tom at 5 o'clock in the morning and woke his father.

Thomas George had a gang of friends that he would hang out with and they would sometimes meet up in the cart shed nearby and, if out very late, he would occasionally sleep there to avoid waking his parents: it was the obvious place for Joseph to look first. As soon as he entered the shed, he saw someone lying on the floor and in seconds realised all was not well. The person was lying on his left side on top of a hurdle or fence surrounded by blood.

Despite searching for his son and finding a body where he thought he might be, Joseph George failed initially to recognise his own kin. Understandably, he was shocked at the sight and ran from the shed without looking any closer. By now the village was waking up and preparing for work. The first local George met was a neighbour, Henry Hillier, who was lacing up his boots at his cottage door, situated not far from the cart shed. 'As soon as I saw him,' George later recalled, 'I said Hen, for God's sake come up, for Fred is beat almost to death!' They returned to the shed together, and Hillier announced the awful truth. 'It's poor Tom; he's cut his throat at last!'

Word was starting to spread around the village about the death and just before 6 o'clock, James Charlton, another young labourer, saw the body and reported Henry Hillier was there crying and saying Tom George had cut his throat and that it was all to do with a girl called Eliza. Hillier then searched under the body and found a knife. He asked George if it was his son's knife, and he said that it was. The body was taken home, where George's sister-in-law washed it, noting the neckerchief was cut in three or four places, but also that there was no blood on the victim's hands or the sleeves of his smock coat, as would be expected if it was suicide. Superstition though, dictated that Tom's knife be broken, so it could not harm anyone else and Joseph George did this before placing it in the coffin; it was retrieved later and taken as evidence.

An inquest was held at the village inn, the George, the following day, Friday 5 April 1850, although the coroner would not allow a proper post-mortem, as he was afraid the cost would not be met by the magistrates. The jury, therefore, recorded on open verdict of 'found dead'. The funeral took place the same day, in Nunney church (sadly, the site of the grave is now lost) and a death certificate issued stating the cause of death as 'Throat cut by whom no evidence to show'. On the Monday, however, the medical officer for Nunney, with assistance from a Frome surgeon, carried out a proper examination, the corpse having been retrieved from its coffin:

> *There was a wound in the throat about 4 inches in length on the left side extending down to the spine bone and so deep that the gullet, windpipe and carotid artery had been severed. The knife had scraped the bone at the back of the neck almost severing the head. There were marks on the bone showing that the wound had been produced by 2 cuts, I believe the wound was commenced by a cut on the left side. If the deceased had inflicted the first cut it would have been impossible for him to have inflicted the second. There was a gash on the forehead of about 1.5 inches cut right down to the bone, it appeared to have been inflicted with a heavy blunt instrument, I found the bone was fractured. The immediate effect of such a blow would be to stun the person receiving it, and most probably it would ultimately have produced death. In my opinion, this blow was given before the throat was cut.*

The victim had not died by his own hand, but had been subjected to a vicious and determined attack. Thomas George had been murdered. The local authority decided they did not have the resources to investigate the case properly and so they called for assistance from London.

The Detective Force had existed for eight years, having come into being as a new department in the capital's Metropolitan Police force in June 1842. Within two months of its inception, it had become fully operational, consisting initially of two inspectors and six sergeants who were tasked with the job of 'infiltrating and detecting crime'. Their headquarters at Great Scotland Yard meant they effectively became part of 'A' Division, which covered the Whitehall district, but what made them different to their uniformed colleagues was the fact they could operate across divisional boundaries and in plain clothes. They could also be hired out to undertake detection work anywhere in the country.

Although the name of the detective who arrived in Nunney to investigate the case has been lost in time, there are only a certain number of possibilities. In April 1850, there were still only eight members of the branch and these included Jonathan 'Jack' Whitcher, who a decade later would investigate the Road Hill House (although in 1850 he was still six years off promotion to Inspector), Henry Smith, who the next year would come to Frome for the Sarah Watts murder, in West Woodlands, and Inspector Field (who would become the inspiration for Charles Dickens's detective in *Bleak House*).

Whichever detective was dispatched to Nunney, they soon determined that whoever hit Tom over the head had then searched his pockets for his knife. His breeches and waistcoat were unbuttoned; his pocket watch had been torn off and on the outside of his right-hand pocket was the bloody hand print of three fingers, with more blood on the inside of his left-hand pocket.

A suspect was quickly apprehended: none other than Henry Hillier; 30-year-old Hillier was a local farm labourer who lived in the village with his wife and children. For some unknown reason he also went by the name of Henry Ashford, Axford or Oxford, and it was Hillier who had not only claimed to have found the knife, but first proposed the suicide theory. He was taken into custody on suspicion of the murder and remanded for ten days. A man named Frederick Phillips was also arrested on suspicion of involvement.

The first full hearing of the case began before Reverend G. Rous and a bench of magistrates at Frome Magistrates Court on Thursday 18 April 1850, and here, the story began to be revealed. Another Hoddinott employee, William Whittaker, who lived on the Frome Road had gone to Hillier's cottage for supper on the evening before the murder. Hillier next went to The Crown Inn, in the Market Place, where he spoke to his brother, Solomon, and asked him not to go to the barn to sleep that night, because 'master was kicking up a row about it'. At a later hearing, the Hoddinotts denied ever having complained about workers sleeping in the barn that year. Hillier then went to Thomas George's cottage and spoke to his mother, Mary, asking her if Joseph (the father) was going muck spreading the following day, implying he would be doing it himself and therefore Joseph would not be needed (an unusual statement, in retrospect, as Hillier had no control over what anyone else's work would be). The dung cart used for muck spreading, however, was kept in the cart shed where the body was found the next morning. Mary asked Hillier if he had seen her son, but he replied he had not. At the hearing, Mary George added that the two often went out together.

Nothing else is known about Henry Hillier's movements that evening until about 10.30 p.m., when he returned home. His wife had been a widow and had a 13-year-old illegitimate son, William Charlton. All three slept in the same room, which was a common practice at the time.

In his evidence, William Charlton stated that,

> *On the 3rd of April I got home from work at about 6.30 and found mother and prisoner who I call father, and William Whittaker, were there – they were at supper. I went to bed leaving the three downstairs. My mother came up for the baby. I went to sleep and awoke at about half past ten. I did not hear the clock strike while I was awake. I heard two persons speaking, mother and father, and another voice sounding like that of Mr Phillips. After that I heard some person go out of the house. I awoke in the night and heard father come to bed. My mother came up just behind him. When they came into the room my mother asked Henry to tell her where he had been and he said he would not. She asked him twice and he gave the same answer.*
>
> *He had a smock coat on. I observed a little blood on the sleeves and on the bosom. He took off the smock and threw it under the bed. The next morning, I woke up before my father and saw my*

mother carry the smock downstairs and when I got down I saw her fetch out a pan of cold water. She did not do anything with the pan and water while I was there. The smock frock was dirty when I saw it. I told my master what I had seen about a week afterwards. I told Thomas Porch before him sometime the same week. I did not hear of any Coroner's Inquest being held.

The committal proceedings concluded with the judge deciding there was sufficient evidence for the case to be tried at the next Assize. The other accused, Phillips, was discharged and young William Charlton was committed to Shepton Mallet prison for his own protection.

The case proper opened at the Crown Court in Wells on the 12 August 1850 before Mr Justice Coleridge. A fellow farm worker, William Norris, produced a stake with hair on it which had been found in the shed. He told the court that,

There were three stakes laying near the hurdle, one of which had clotted hair on it. I cut some hair from the head of the deceased and compared it with the hair on the stake; they were of the same colour, and I cannot see any difference between them. The stake was found against the wall of the shed, about five or six yards from the body.

So far, the question of motive seems not to have been mentioned. There were rumours that a number of those involved in the case belonged to a gang of sheep rustlers and that Thomas George had threatened to tell what he knew.

William Charlton was then called and gave the same damning evidence as he had before the magistrates. But upon cross-examination by Mr Edwards, Henry Hillier's counsel, he was asked certain questions, to which he replied:

I said before the magistrates that I heard the clock strike but that is not true. I also said that I heard two speaking downstairs and one of them sounded like Frederick Phillips and that I heard someone go out of the house and lock the door but none of that is true.

Charlton went on to contradict nearly all the other statements contained in his depositions before the magistrates. After a great deal of prevarication, the boy admitted he had been told by his master that there had been blood on his father's smock and had simply repeated it. The prosecution case was falling apart and the judge stepped in.

'Did you see any smock at all when your father came to bed on this night?' asked the Judge. 'No, I did not,' answered William Charlton.

At this point, Hillier's defence lawyer Mr Edwards had a meeting with prosecutor Phinn and suggested the case be abandoned because the main prosecution witness could not be relied upon. They agreed to consult the judge who, suspecting the family had pressurised the boy into retracting his evidence, wanted to know more. Directing Charlton to step forward he asked him,

'*How long before you went before the magistrates did you know that you were going there?*'

'*I did not know I was going there until I was taken,*' the boy replied.

'*After you were examined by the magistrates did you ever go back to your home?*'

'*No, sir.*'

'*Did you know whether your father-in-law or mother know that you were going to be taken before the magistrates?*'

'*No sir.*'

'*At what place were you taken?*'

'*At Pitsford.*'

His lordship then retired to consult a colleague and on his return decided to continue, as he deemed there was enough evidence to go before a jury. Witnesses were called to give evidence on comments made by Hillier.

Maria Stride gave evidence that,

> *About 2 months back, when in Messer's Hoddinotts brewhouse I heard Henry Hilliar say, 'I wish Tom George was dead; that someone would kill him out of the way. I can't bear the sight of him on the farm,' and the Saturday after Tom died he said he trembled so much that he could scarce stand since Tom was killed.*

Thomas Knapton knew victim and accused well and stated that,

> *Sometime before the murder I saw Henry in his garden and he said he wished Tom George was dead and stiff, out of his sight, for he could not bear to see him about. About a month after that I was again in the garden and Henry and I were talking about Tom George and how Henry had been terrifying him. He said that Tom George told him that he would as soon do himself a mischief as not.*

Other witnesses talked of Henry constantly cursing and swearing at Thomas and declaring that he would beat him.

Hillier's family continued to be unhelpful to his cause. Next up was his sister Sophia, who gave evidence that,

> *On 31 March I lent Henry a smock-frock, as I have done several times before. He generally returned the frock dirty, but this time it had been washed & ironed. There were some stains on it that were not there when I lent it. When I asked him, Henry told me he had spilt some cider over it.*

Constable Ivey, from Frome, then produced the smock coat; it was he that had arrested Hillier and had sent it to William Herapath, an analytical chemist, for examination. Herapath though, could find no trace of blood on the garment.

At the close of the prosecution's case, the judge requested the jury to ignore the evidence of William Charlton, Hillier's 13-year-old stepson, and consider the case without his statement: was there still enough to convict? The jury deliberated and decided that there wasn't. They returned a verdict of 'Not Guilty'.

The judge stated he agreed with the jury's decision, but said that the coroner was negligent in not immediately carrying out a post-mortem, to save money. Had that been carried out properly, he said, the verdict might either have been very different or the case not brought at all. So, did he, or didn't he? It certainly seems Henry Hillier thoroughly disliked Thomas George, but that is not the same as deciding to murder him.

A couple of points stand out, however. The main blow was to Thomas George's forehead and cheek, implying his assailant was facing him when the assault took place. This meant they could have been arguing, which would suggest they knew each other and had something to argue about. George was not ambushed or struck from behind as might be expected in a case of simple robbery, and as the wounds were to the left of the head, it might be inferred that the murderer was right-handed.

The evidence also states Thomas George's pocket watch was torn off, but not that it was stolen. The chances are that the perpetrator and George had met and argued. There was a brief struggle, during which the pocket watch was broken, and then the victim was smashed on the head with a fence post that rendered him unconscious. As he lay on the ground, the assailant made sure he was dead by slitting his throat.

As to the murderer's reasons, whether it was Henry Hillier or not, we will never know, but it seems the locals knew a lot more about it than came out in court. Apart from rumours about George threatening to spill the beans on sheep stealing, there does not seem to have been any motive.

Once William Charlton changed his story, it meant the prosecution's main witness had gone and Justice Coleridge thought there was insufficient evidence for the case to continue, therefore he effectively stopped the trial half way through. It is often said the defence case is the highlight of the prosecution case, meaning skilful cross-examination of the defendant and his witnesses will often prove their undoing, exposing facts the prosecution did not pick up on before. Rightly or wrongly, the judge did not allow the trial to continue and Hillier was never asked why he said the things he was alleged to have said about Tom George.

The Hillier family left, or were obliged to leave, Nunney after the court case; it is more than likely that many were convinced of his guilt and would not employ him or his family. By March the following year they were all in the Frome Workhouse. Somehow though, they turned their lives around, because by the 1861 census they were living – with two more children – at The Butts in Frome, a short distance from the Red Lion public house, where in the same year Hillier had his altercation with Davis about his unsavoury past and uttered the immortal words: 'Take care, for thee dost not know.'

CHAPTER 10

Going Off The Rails

The mysterious misadventure of George Taylor, 1857

On an ordinary Thursday night in August 1857, the *Leopold*, the 10 o'clock mail train from Weymouth, was rapidly approaching Frome. The two-engine GWR express had been late leaving Bruton, but had now gone through Witham and was one and half miles from its next stop. What happened next was both tragic and mysterious; leaving many questions unanswered to this day.

Frederick Somers, the *Leopold*'s guard, was on his break and leaning on a window in the first carriage. Something caught his attention and the next moment he saw a figure fall from the train's tender onto a wall and then rebound against the carriage he was in. As quickly as Somers could, he blew the whistle to raise the alarm, went outside of the carriage, and then made his way along the tender to inform the fireman. Once alerted, the train slowly came to a halt.

Somers and Handy ran back along the track and found their driver, George Taylor, lying on the left bank of Bull's Bridge. He was conscious and managed to say that he thought his back was broken, but said nothing about how the accident had occurred. It was later agreed by those involved that he was completely sober. While the first engine was uncoupled and made its way to Frome to inform them what had happened, the driver was picked up by his fellow-workers and placed into a second-class carriage. He was taken to a local public house, under the care of Dr White and Mr J. Portch – a postal worker waiting for the mail on board the train – but died soon afterwards. How he had met his fate would now be up to those at the inquest to determine.

The railways had come to Frome seven years earlier, in October 1850. An Act of Parliament in 1845 had given rise to the Wilts, Somerset & Weymouth Railway Company, whose ambition was to open several routes, including a Westbury to Weymouth line that would pass through Frome. Isambard Kingdom Brunel was appointed engineer of the line and construction began soon after the act had been passed.

By 1848 however, an economic depression had arrived. Loans, for the most part, were no longer available and calls on shares went unpaid. This affected many of the numerous railway schemes, including the WS&W and, with the company having run out of money, it was up to the Great Western Railway to step in and finance its completion. The WS&W, although seemingly independent, was really part of GWR, having been set up with the hope that a local sounding concern would attract more subscriptions. With this façade now shed, the GWR took over construction of the Westbury to Frome section in March 1850. The WS&W was no more and would eventually be dissolved.

Although the financial outlook remained unsettled, the larger company possessed greater resources and so the GWR was soon able to begin work on the line again and gave it top priority in the hope a lucrative trade would be forthcoming from the nearby Somerset coalfields. Once this section was given the go-ahead, land had to be repurchased and new lands acquired. One of the men from Frome who sold land to the railway company was local magistrate and businessman John Sinkins. He also owned the land on which Frome station was to be built and after this had been bought from him, construction work began at the start of August 1850. Such was GWR's desire to open the line as quickly as possible that the station had been virtually completed by the end of that month. The line between Westbury and Frome was finally opened on 7 October 1850.

By the time the line was completed, talk of extending it on to Weymouth had all but ceased. In 1852 though, another Act of Parliament was obtained by the GWR, giving the impetus to take the line all the way. Once more, they believed a more local sounding name would fare better when raising funds and so the 'Frome, Yeovil and Weymouth Railway' company was born. Sadly, like the WS&W before it, it was unsuccessful and short-lived; the GWR having to take back the reins and finance the line itself, while the subsidiary company was dissolved in all but name.

By the autumn of 1856 the line had been extended another twenty-six miles, passing through the stations of Witham, Bruton, Castle Cary, Sparkford and Marston, before it reached Yeovil.

Frome Railway Station, which opened in 1850, seven years before George Taylor's tragic and fatal fall from the Weymouth train on its way to Frome. (FSLS)

As with the Westbury to Frome section, this was a single line with five trains a day in each direction. A few months later, the ultimate objective was achieved when the outskirts of the coastal town were reached. The line between Weymouth and Westbury eventually became operational on 20 January 1857, a mere eight months before the tragic events of 13 August.

Everything had seemed normal when the *Leopold* left Weymouth on that Thursday evening, and remained so for most of the journey. Not long after the train left Bruton station however, George Taylor turned to his fireman, Miles Handy, and told him to keep a look out on things for a while. The driver then made his way back along the engine, towards the tender and the carriages behind. Handy assumed he was going back to check there was enough water to get them through to Chippenham (their ultimate destination) without taking on more.

Not long afterwards, one of the lamps had gone out and Handy was trying to re-light it when he heard a whistle and then a shout from the guard to say a person had fallen overboard. He shut off the steam and signalled to the driver of the engine in front to tell him something was amiss. As Handy would soon discover, the unfortunate victim was none other than his driver, George Taylor.

The inquest into the incident took place two days later, at a public house, in Frome, and a somewhat strange tale indeed would emerge. The use of such places for inquests was a common practice. Within many communities, especially rural ones, inns or public houses were often the only readily available indoor spaces large enough for such proceedings to take place. The establishments were also likely to have a sizeable table big enough to hold a body for viewing by the jury and for post-mortems to be performed. The proceedings would normally be held upstairs or in a back room, sometimes with their own entrances so that the coroner and others in attendance need not pass through the public areas.

This arrangement was more than acceptable to the landlords of these places. They would earn extra money not only by hiring out the room but, dependent on the nature of the crime, would enjoy increased custom during breaks of the proceedings, with witnesses, jurors, reporters and magisterial professionals no doubt quenching their thirst, along with inquisitive locals trying to slake their curiosity. It can be assumed though that it was not always the most congenial of surroundings, as the sounds of conviviality and the smell of alcohol and tobacco smoke would surely percolate through to where the inquest was taking place.

Although similar to a criminal trial, inquests were presided over by a coroner, rather than a magistrate and in this case, it was the coroner for East Somerset, Daniel Ashford, who oversaw proceedings. Ashford had travelled from nearby Shepton Mallet, where the 49-year-old had a legal practice. He had taken over the coroner's position from his father around seven years earlier. Verdicts would be decided by a jury, which consisted of twelve 'able and sufficient men', who had all received warrants to attend. Unlike a criminal trial at that time, jurors had the right to ask questions.

The first witness called was the 34-year-old Sarah Fouraker, who had been a passenger on the Weymouth train, having boarded at Yeovil. Sarah was a native of Frome, but had married Thomas Fouraker, seventeen years her senior and the Inspector of Police in Exeter, where they had a house in the High Street. The account she gave to the coroner was that on the evening of Thursday 13 August she was travelling from Exeter to Frome and had to change at Yeovil to pick up the Frome train at 11 o'clock. She was alone in the second carriage from the tender when Taylor looked in and asked her if she wanted 'company'. She told the inquest she had said 'no'. He told her that there was no one in the next carriage and that he would keep her company; then he tried to kiss her but she refused and so he went towards the door as though to leave, but returned several times asking her to shake hands. She made it perfectly clear that she wanted nothing to do with him and kept her face turned to the window, so as not look at him.

Mrs Fouraker then said that she had seen,

> *nothing more of the deceased till he was picked up from the bank on the left hand side of the train. He left the carriage on the right hand side. I did not then know who he was. When he was in the carriage he seemed very much frightened because I told him that I would expose him. Shortly after he left the whistle blew and the train stopped. He appeared to be sober and not like a man who had been drinking.*

One the jurors asked her why she hadn't raised the alarm at the time, to which she replied she was much too frightened to do so and besides, Taylor had not used any violence towards her or pushed her.

Frederick Somers, the Great Western Railway guard, was then called. He took the oath, sat down, and began his testimony:

> *I am guard on the Great Western Railway, and acted as such on Thursday to the 10 o'clock train from Weymouth. We were rather later starting from Bruton that night. When about a mile and half from Witham towards Frome, I saw the deceased fall from the tender against a wall, and rebound against the carriage I was sitting in, which broke the panel of the door. I was leaning on the window of the carriage at the time. I endeavoured to stop the train as soon as possible, by blowing my whistle, and went along the tender, and told the stoker. We went back and found the deceased by the side of Bull's Bridge, where he had fallen; he was sensible. He made no remark as to how the accident happened. Deceased was sober. Before leaving Weymouth, his mother brought him some coffee. My break was in the first carriage, from the tender about two and half yards.*

Mr J. Portch was then called. He worked for the post office (he would later become the town's postmaster) and had been waiting to collect the mail from the train at Frome Station; along with Dr White, he was with George Taylor when he died. He said:

> *I was at the Frome station awaiting the arrival of the mail train from Weymouth when the first engine arrived, and I heard that a man had fallen off the engine or tender. I went for Dr White, and afterwards assisted in conveying the deceased to the Nicoll Arms. I stayed with him till his death, which took place at 1 o'clock on Friday morning.*

It seems from the contemporary newspaper reports that there were no further questions asked or witnesses called. Was Mrs Fouraker not questioned too closely because of who her husband was? Did she tell Taylor that her husband was a policeman, which caused him to seem 'very much frightened'? Did the fear of losing his job make him so nervous he missed his footing and fell from his own train, or indeed, did he deliberately step away from the tender through the shame of what he had done? Or was there a lot more to the whole situation? We will never know.

Bull's Bridge, where George Taylor was found after falling from the Weymouth train. (Authors' Collection)

The jury brought in a verdict of 'accidental death' and the deceased left a widow and two small children.

A small footnote to this case is the location of the accident, Bull's Bridge, where George Taylor lay fatally injured after falling from the train. The farm adjacent to the bridge, and in fact the railway line ran through its land, was called Battle Farm. And it was here, sometime during the afternoon of Wednesday 24 September 1851, almost six years earlier, that 14-year-old Sarah Watts was brutally raped and murdered by an unknown assailant.

Chapter 11

A Crime of Passion?

George Britten and the Woolverton Murder, 1867

Possibly one of the most callous and calculated acts in the annals of crime in Frome and its surrounding area occurred at Woolverton on Saturday 20 July 1867. Around four o'clock in the morning George Rogers noticed smoke coming from a malt house that belonged to 51-year-old George Britten. Rogers was on his way to work but he quickly ran back home to alert his father and a neighbour, before returning to Britten's thatched cottage, where the owner lived with his wife Martha and young son, Charles. As the outbuilding was situated only about 15ft from the cottage, Rogers ran up the garden path and knocked loudly on the door several times to raise the alarm, but to no avail. Even when he threw gravel at the upstairs window, there was no answer.

Eventually, after what seemed like an age to Rogers, there was a slight movement in one of the upstairs windows and the owner peered out into the dawning light. As Britten got dressed, Rogers returned to the malt house to try and tackle the fire. By now, several neighbours were on the scene and together they forced the malt house door open.

Despite the potential severity of the situation, George Britten did not seem to be too concerned about it. Not only did he take an age to come downstairs, but once outside he tried everything in his power to disrupt the attempts of Rogers and the others to put out the fire. He insisted that the malt-house door, which had been forced open, be shut lest the draught make the fire worse. As it transpired, this was an attempt to make sure the corpse he had put in there earlier was not seen. He was too late though, as several of those present had noticed it on a board, atop a pile of coke. Britten then stepped inside the malt house and in his quest to take a closer look at the body had 'accidentally' knocked it off its resting place and into the flames.

By now, news of the fire had reached the police station in Frome, about four miles away, and Superintendent Deggan had dispatched the Frome Volunteer Fire Brigade (FVFB) to Woolverton, along with one of his constables, PC Chandler. On their arrival, the fire was swiftly extinguished by the FVFB, but on discovery of the charred body, the police constable sent for his superior.

Superintendent Edward Deggan had been born in Bristol, of Irish parents, and reached his present rank before the age of 32. Prior to arriving in Frome in October 1860 he had been stationed at Axbridge, located at the other end of Somerset, near the coastal towns of Burnham-on-Sea and Weston-super-Mare. He lived permanently at the police station in Christchurch Street West – which had been built a decade earlier to a design by Major Charles Davis, the city architect for Bath – with his wife, son and two daughters.

When Superintendent Deggan arrived at the Woolverton malt house, he was informed by PC Chandler that the body was thought to be of a tramp who, it was suggested, had broken in and accidently started the fire. On closer inspection though, Deggan found several items of clothing which had not perished in the flames. These included a bonnet and pairs of stockings, which led him to the conclusion that the body was female. And what was more, blood matted into the victim's hair which, despite the fire, had also survived more-or-less intact, revealed to the police officer that the woman lying before him had been murdered, most likely before the fire had begun.

George Britten was now asked if he could identify the corpse. He answered that he could not. Even when it was pointed out to him the resemblance between the dead woman and his wife – both had two very protruding front teeth, a similarity many of the neighbours there had already commented on – Britten insisted the body was not that of his spouse telling Deggan that she was away visiting friends at West Pennard. So fully convinced were the neighbours that the dead person was Martha Britten, that Deggan requested her husband look again, paying particular attention this time to the teeth and hair. To help him, the Superintendent even carefully lifted the head so he could better see the teeth. 'I cannot recognise her,' Britten insisted, but the charade was quickly disintegrating, as he was trembling uncontrollably as he said it. Finally, Britten caved in and admitted the body was that of his wife, Martha. He was immediately arrested by Superintendent Deggan and charged with her wilful murder, as well as setting fire to the malt house.

George Britten was escorted to Frome Police Station and placed in one of the cells. As well as the magistrates' court, which had moved from its location at the end of Edgell's Lane in the town centre, there were several cells, making the guardhouse next to The Blue Boar and the blind house, in St John's churchyard, redundant.

On his arrival at the police station, Britten said very little, other than 'It's a bad job.' When his brother-in-law, a Mr Woolly visited him the next day though, it seemed he had more to say, although preferred to write it down on a note which he tried to surreptitiously hand to Woolly. Superintendent Deggan, having noticed this covert transaction, took possession of the paper, which was revealed to be a half-finished confession of the murder by Britten.

Perhaps realising he now had nothing left to hide, Britten asked for the paper back and then continued where he had left off. In part, the statement read:

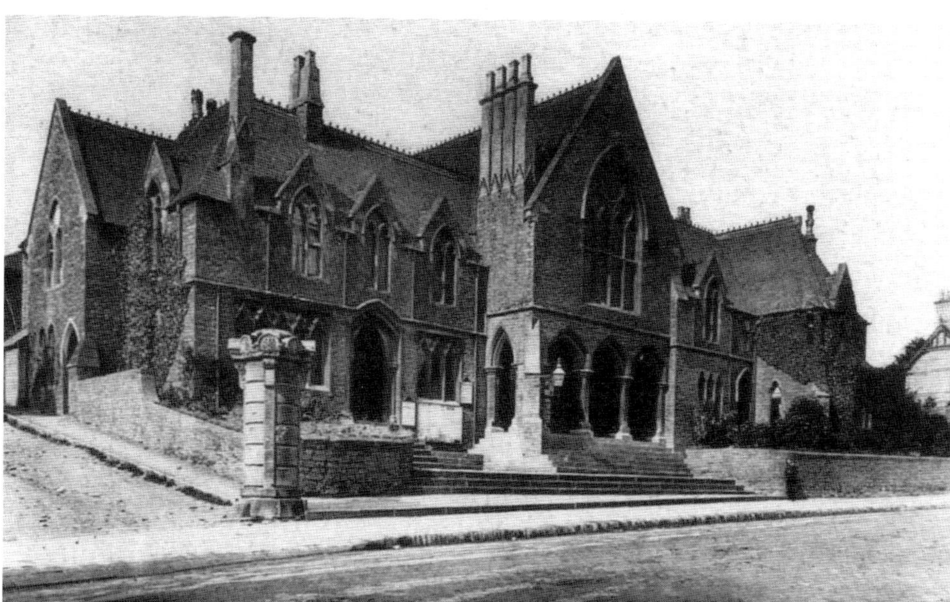

Frome Police Station where George Britten was taken after being arrested.

With shame and true abhorrence and repentance of the deed I have done, I confess it was I that foully murdered my poor wife. It was done in the heat of passion and in a fit of jealousy and arose thus; I saw what I shall keep to myself, told her of it; she treated it lightly, which enraged me. I caught of the first thing that came to hand, struck her with it three or four times … Oh, what power the Devil must have had over me.

The inquest on Martha Britten was held two days later, on Monday 22 July 1867, at the Red Lion Inn, in Woolverton. As was the normal procedure, a jury was present and its foreman was the Reverend Baker. The coroner in attendance was the one for East Somerset, Dr Wybrants. According to the later newspaper reports, the room was crowded with onlookers. Although not able to intercede, which, as was the usual practice, Frome solicitor, Mr Messiter, watched the proceedings on behalf of the prisoner's family. George Britten was also present and the newspapers described him as 'a somewhat aged man, grey-haired, and dressed in a suit of black'.

Along with Superintendent Deggan was his superior, the chief constable of Somerset, Mr Valentine Goold. The latter informed the jury that as the prisoner had confessed, the proceedings would be considerably shortened. Nevertheless, witnesses would be called and the first of these was the labourer George Rogers.

Rogers took the stand and recounted his journey to work, the discovery of the fire, and his actions in trying to awaken Britten. He also recalled Britten's behaviour, when he came downstairs and entered the malt house, including tipping his wife's body into the fire, off the board upon which it had been lying.

Several of Britten's neighbours were then called. These included Mr James Parsons, a farmer, who, along with several others, had laid the body of Martha Britten on a sack and removed it to another part of the malt house before the police had arrived. Others, such as Sarah Prescott and Mary Pickford, the latter the Britten's next-door neighbour, gave testimonies as to when they had last seen the victim alive and that they had no hesitation as to identifying her as the deceased. They also gave insights into the marriage, which seemed to suggest an affectionate and loving one.

A Henry Parsons then took the witness stand. He was one of the Beckington surgeons, along with his son, who had carried out the post-mortem on Martha Britten. He stated, under oath, that:

I made a post-mortem examination of the body on Saturday afternoon. The body was that of a woman rather above the middle height, well-nourished, in good condition, and between 40 and 50 years old. It had evidently been subjected to intense heat. The skin was extensively burnt, and in many places cracked, and in some instances the bones appeared through the skin and the muscles were exposed. The burns were most severe about the right thigh, up the groin, and the calves of the legs. The abdomen and chest were also much burnt, the right side of the face was also burnt and blackened, but the left side and scalp were comparatively uninjured.

The forehead was burnt and blackened on the right side, but less so on the left side. In the centre of the forehead, close beneath the roots of the hair, was a deep contused wound about one inch and a half in length horizontal, but curved into the convex downwards. On the left temple, there was another lacerated wound, the edges ragged and gaping. On some of the hairs round this wound I perceived small clots of blood. The skin about this was unburnt. About two inches behind this towards the back of the head there was a large wound. This was a V shape, the apex backward, and each line of the wound about two inches in length, the flap between the two being loose. The hair behind the wound was clotted with blood, the clots being bright red in colour and soft, probably from exposure to heat. The edges of the wound were blackened and burnt.

The cause of death was the blow on the head, but I cannot say which. On dissecting the scalp there was an effusion of blood between the integuments and the bone. The effusion was greater in front, corresponding with the wound and in the back of the head. The brain was not congested but pale, and there was also a laceration in two parts. The skull was not fractured. The cause of death was concussion of the brain from a blow or blows.

In answer to questions by the chief constable and others, Parsons replied that he believed several blows had been administered by a blunt instrument, such as a hammer, and Martha Britten had been dead when she was burnt. He had formed this opinion, he said, as he could not see blisters on any part of the body. Although he could not give an exact time between death and burning, he believed the victim had not been dead for any longer than two days.

It was then Superintendent Deggan's turn to give his testimony and he recalled the sequence of events from when he had been called to Woolverton, to arresting the prisoner and bringing him back to Frome police station. He then produced the 'confession', which had been written by Britten the previous day. It was addressed to Martha Britten's brother, Mr Woolly, who was with the prisoner at the time:

> *Mr. Woolly, I do to you what I could not to anyone else. With shame and true abhorrence and repentance of the deed I have done, I confess it was I that foully murdered my poor wife. It was done in the heat of passion and in a fit of jealousy, and arose thus. I saw what I shall keep to myself – told her of it – she treated it lightly, which enraged me. I caught hold of the first thing that came to hand. Struck her with it three or four times. Oh, how I wish I had been blind or God had struck me dead before I did so! Oh, what power the devil must have over me! It seemed as though I had almost a hundred devils in me, and I believe, had twenty people been there, I should, had they interfered, served them in a similar manner; but after it was done and I reflected a little time, oh, how I detested and deplored this act, viewed it with abhorrence and, oh, what I would have gave to bring her to life again!*
>
> *I fully intended then to have destroyed myself, but was prevented by two thoughts – first, that alone in the house, the child would come down and first find us and no doubt would lose his reason or something as bad. Second, that probably God may forgive murder even, but not self-murder. Then I thought of at once giving myself up, but then the devil or my own evil heart tempted and induced me to try and hide my act from the world, which I did immediately by carrying her poor body over the wall by the pear tree into the malt house, and finished the next night.*
>
> *Once you said if anything happened to me you would take care of the boy – will you do so now? There is a draft on the Old Bristol bank for £350 in my trunk. Do so for not mine but his sake, and I hope, poor fellow, he may reward you. Oh, what I have brought on myself and friends, and first begun and ended by false friends, which has been my bane through life. Oh, how I pity and feel for poor Elizabeth, you, your family, my boy, Charles, and Joseph.*

> *As for myself, now I feel my doom is fixed, and that since the last tragedy I deserve it, but not before. I have no wish to live. May God receive my wife's soul in his abode above, and may he forgive me and receive mine at last also. And for man, I do not ask nor expect to receive forgiveness. Do let me again beg you and poor Elizabeth to take the poor boy into your care, and may God bless you all and him.*

Deggan then continued and repeated what Britten told him, he said, after writing the statement.

> *I killed her on Thursday night, I put her body in two sacks. I tied a rope round her neck. I dragged her body up the ladder by the pear tree, threw it over the tiles, dragged it over the plank that was over the cistern, and then set fire to the place. Oh, God forgive me! I loved her. I struck her with a piece of lead downstairs.*

It did not take the jury long to return a verdict of 'Wilful murder' and George Britten then had to appear at Frome petty sessions, where he was committed for trial at the next Somerset Assizes.

The assize court in England and Wales was normally held twice a year, Lent and summer. These courts were under the control and organisation of the Clerks of the Assize. Judges would travel around several neighbouring counties, at the set times, to hear cases and administer justice. This gave rise to the 'circuits' and in England, by the mid-nineteenth century, there were a total of six: Home, Norfolk, Midland, Northern, Oxford and Western. Each circuit included anything between four and eight counties and when the assizes were in session, each would be visited in rotation, with a certain number of days allotted for it.

Woolverton, being in Somerset, came under the jurisdiction of the Western Circuit, which also contained Hampshire, Wiltshire, Dorset, Devon, and Cornwall. The next assizes after Britten's committal in Frome was the one held in summer. He therefore appeared before Mr Justice Willes, at Wells on 7 August 1867, charged with murdering his wife with malice aforethought.

The opening of a session was always accompanied by a great amount of ceremony, with the under-sheriff meeting the judges at the county boundary, after which they entered the town with an escort of javelin men and fanfares of trumpets.

Trials at the assize courts would take place in the county in which the crime was committed, with a jury drawn from the same area. At the start of the trial the prisoner would first be 'arraigned' or have the charges read to him and then asked to plead either 'guilty' or 'not guilty' to the charge they faced. If they pleaded not guilty a jury would be chosen from the twenty-four men who had been summoned; these were men between 21 and 60 years old who had certain property qualifications, quite often they were shopkeepers or small landowners. The accused had the right to object to individual jurors, if they had good reason, but once everyone was satisfied, the jury was officially empanelled and the trial began with an opening speech by the prosecuting barrister.

On hearing the charge read out, Britten was asked how he pleaded. The prisoner replied, 'Guilty of the act but not with malice aforethought.' The judge took this as a plea of 'Not Guilty' and allowed the prosecution to begin its case.

The prosecutor, Mr Saunders, began by addressing the jury regarding the publicity that had appeared in the newspapers. He told them that there had been so much, in fact, he would not be surprised if an opinion – as to the prisoner's guilt or innocence – had already been formed by many, if not all of them. But, he said, they must focus solely on the evidence that was about to be presented and not be swayed by any preconceptions.

Saunders then warned them that the defence would aim to convince them that the prisoner should be found guilty of manslaughter rather than murder, as his wife had been killed 'in the heat of passion'. No one would be happier than he if the jury did indeed find Britten guilty of manslaughter, but he reminded the jury that Martha Britten had been hit over the head several times, not just once, as might be expected of the type of crime the defence were pleading. Medical evidence would back this key point up.

As per the inquest, the labourer George Rogers, who had been the one to raise the alarm, was called as the first witness and he was followed onto the stand by several of George Britten's neighbours. And, like the inquest, the evidence slowly mounted up against the prisoner, showing him to have behaved in a calculated manner throughout the whole sordid business of killing his wife, trying to dispose of her body and then denying her identity once she had been discovered.

The defence – led by a Mr Prideaux and a Mr Folkard – now had the chance to put their case. As the prosecutor had expected, they argued that Martha Britten's murder was a crime of passion. George Britten, they said, was a devoted and loving husband who had committed the act in the heat of the moment and on an irresistible impulse.

The jury, having heard both sides, took less than three minutes to come down on the side of the prosecution and find George Britten guilty of wilful murder; the deciding factor, as was later revealed, being the undeniable and wholly premeditated fact that the prisoner had attempted to dispose of his wife and evidence surrounding her murder by starting a fire. Britten accepted his death sentence and seemed to show less emotion as it was pronounced than the judge.

If the inquest and subsequent trial had become spectacles in the eyes of the public and sensationalised by the press, the prison authorities were determined to do their utmost to ensure George Britten's execution would pass as uneventfully as possible. With that in mind, his execution was set for Thursday 29 August 1867, and would take place at Taunton, but those that knew it were sworn to utmost secrecy.

The custom for executions at Taunton was usually a Tuesday and on that day, 27 August, a rumour circulated that Britten would be hanged then, a rumour validated by a press report. The assembled spectators were therefore disappointed when it did not materialise, as were those who turned up the following day.

At 1 o'clock in the morning of 29 August 1867, the erection of the gallows began. Newspapers speculated later that the sound of the hammering by the workmen as they constructed the apparatus must have resounded through the still night and no doubt reached the cell of the condemned man. What was certain is that sometime before George Britten was led out into the morning light, dressed all in black, he was visited by prison chaplain, Reverend Howse.

The mournful procession then set out in the direction of the scaffold. On reaching it, the condemned prisoner was met by his executioner, 66-year-old William Calcraft. Calcraft was one of the most prolific of British executioners and it is estimated that during his nearly five-decade stint as official executioner for the City of London he carried out 450 executions. On this day, he was also dressed in black, wore a showy gold albert chain and had a flower in the button-hole of his coat.

Due to the secrecy surrounding the execution, it was estimated that only around 3,000 people, mostly locals of Taunton, were in attendance. It may sound an incredible number from our perspective, but Calcraft and his fellow executioners regularly carried out their morbid occupation in front of 30,000 spectators.

George Britten followed the reverend up the gallows steps and almost instinctively placed himself beneath the main beam. With everything ready, Britten now thanked the reverend and officials for their kindness and attention, shook hands with them as well as with his executioner, and then prepared to meet his maker. Although efforts had been made to secure a reprieve it was unsuccessful. The condemned man received the news with his customary lack of emotion, saying that he was ready to die for what he had done. Calcraft, who had been behind Britten as they ascended the steps, now calmly stepped forward and pulled from his pocket a white cap, which he drew over the prisoner's head. He then produced a rope and slid the noose over Britten's head and down around his neck. The hangman then stood on a stool and threw the other end of the rope over the beam. For a moment or two, he meticulously studied both, calculating the amount of 'slack' that would be required, before passing the rope over the beam once more and tying it off using a double knot.

A few seconds later, the bolt was withdrawn and, as one newspaper reported it, the condemned 'was launched into eternity'. By all accounts, it took some time before his corpse became listless, but eventually, a little after 9.05 a.m., George Britten's life expired and he became the last person to be publicly hanged outside Taunton Gaol.

In the aftermath of the trial, it came to light that George Britten had somewhat of a mysterious past. He had been a farmer and at the time he murdered his wife, was living off the rent from properties he owned. Five years earlier, however, he had simply disappeared. To begin with it was thought he had been murdered, since his bloodstained hat and battered lantern had been found near his home. There had been long-standing rumours of an affair and after his 'disappearance', the woman he was supposed to have been seeing turned up drowned.

As suddenly as he had disappeared, so he reappeared, three years later, the intervening years having been spent in New Zealand, according to what Britten told the wife he had abandoned. It seems Martha forgave him and they picked up the threads of their marriage as if he had never been gone.

In retrospect, this decision cost Martha Britten her life and in light of her murder, rumours began to circulate about the circumstances behind the drowned woman's demise. The truth surrounding her death, and Britten's disappearance, will probably never be known, as the only person who could have shed light on them was the man who met his fate at the end of a rope on 29 August 1867.

Chapter 12

The Cry of War

Frome and the Salvation Army, 1884

It may seem strange today to think of the Salvation Army as anything other than a hymn-singing, charitable organisation full of bonneted old ladies with tambourines, but there was a time when the behaviour of the 'Sally Army' brought them into direct conflict with the law and provoked violent reprisals from local communities.

Towards the end of the nineteenth century, there existed in Frome an increasingly strained relationship between the townspeople and members of the Salvation Army – Salvationists – due to the latter's overtly antagonistic tactics and flagrant disregard of the laws. From isolated acts of violence in the first couple of years of the 1880s, it escalated to more regular skirmishes and culminated, in 1884, in a full-scale riot.

The Salvation Army was formed in London in 1865 by a former Methodist minister, William Booth, and his wife, Catherine, although for the first years of its existence it was known as the East London Christian Mission. Their remit was to bring salvation to the poor and destitute, through administering to their physical and spiritual needs.

In 1878, the Booths decided on a radical overhaul and renamed their mission the Salvation Army; the latter part of the title reflecting the fact that this new organisation was founded on quasi-military lines. This included giving certain members ranks – such as major, captain and lieutenant – along with banners, barracks and brass bands.

The 'Army's' approach was summed up by Booth – who bestowed on himself the title of general – as the three S's: Soup, Soap and Salvation. In pursuit of potential members for their congregation – addicts, prostitutes and alcoholics – their quest took them to places where alcohol was served or sold. This,

The Salvation Army's two biggest foes were the demon drink and the Skeleton Army.

unsurprisingly, brought Booth and his 'soldiers' into conflict with pub landlords and other purveyors of the 'evil' liquid, as well as those souls not wishing to be saved from their vices.

Before long, this opposition to the Salvation Army manifested itself in organised groups that, although localised, quickly became known nationally as the Skeleton Army. In deliberate antagonism, they also based themselves along militaristic lines; their flags were adorned with the skull and crossbones and inscribed, in mockery of the Salvationists' three S's, with three B's: Beef, Beer, and Bacca!

The solitary aim of the Skeleton Armies was to confront and disrupt Salvationists' activities wherever and whenever they surfaced in public. Inevitably, it was only a matter of time before confrontations turned violent. One such incident occurred in January 1882 in Sheffield, where a riot ensued. A year later, another took place in London. As the Salvation Army marched through Bethnal Green, they were pelted by an array of missiles – flour, rotten eggs, stones, bricks – and many of its members were beaten.

It was in the same year as the London incident that the first account of major trouble in Frome was reported. Initially, there had been isolated attacks on members of the Salvation Army in outlying areas of the town, such as Buckland Dinham, but it was not long before this escalated, one Saturday evening in August of 1883, to something much more serious. According to a report in the *Bath Chronicle*:

> *the streets of Frome were in a state of disorder the whole evening. It was announced that the Salvation Army intended having two contingents to visit them on that evening, and that a new banner would be presented, after which the town would be bombarded. A brass band was also expected.*

At the last minute, the Salvationists decided not to march into the centre of town due to the number of locals that had gathered there, no doubt intent on disruption. They satisfied themselves instead with a 'hallelujah tea' at six o'clock in the evening followed by a 'march out' from their barracks in Locks Lane (now Locks Hill) to The Butts and back again. The route they choose took in several back streets, but avoided the main centre. However, the several hundred locals gathered in the Market Place got wind of this change of plan and swiftly made their way en masse to Locks Lane, to lay in wait.

On the Salvation Army's return to Locks Lane, they found the route blocked and were unable to enter their barracks for more than half an hour. Abuse was hurled at them and several were attacked. The police were called and helped the Salvationists to get safely inside their barracks.

The crowd meanwhile, dispersed, only to congregate back in the Market Place. According to the *Chronicle*, there were,

> *nearly two thousand persons being present, many armed with very effective cudgels. Soon after this time the Skeleton Army assembled, with a new banner, which consisted of an immense white sheet with the motto 'Blood and Thunder' surmounting*

> *a very roughly-drawn design of skull and cross-bones. Going away at a swinging march, this Army paraded the town singing very ribald songs. In their wake fireworks were let off …* [all] *over the town, squibs, crackers, and other small fireworks were being let off on Saturday evening, and it was not until nearly ten o'clock that the streets resumed an orderly appearance.*

The following year, saw an even bigger disturbance and a pitched battle. The police had no problem with the Salvation Army – or indeed anyone else – marching through the town, so long as they did not stop and cause obstruction. Despite repeated assurances to the contrary, Salvationists still went out onto the streets of the town, stopped in the middle of busy thoroughfares and began preaching. The result was predictable – either violence from the local populace, or arrest by the police. Two such arrests were made in July 1884 and this would be the spark that would ignite Frome's biggest disturbance of all.

In its edition of Wednesday 16 July 1884, the *Frome Times* reported that,

> *We regret exceedingly that we are once again threatened with those breaches of the law, and with the establishment of another Skeleton Army in Frome. For some time past the officers of the Salvation Army stationed in the town have become more and more aggressive, and, not only this, have violated their pledges given to the police and to the magistrates that they will behave in conformity with the law. The fact has been that for a long time past there has been a strained relationship between the people of Frome and the Army, and this has been brought about by the evasion of the law on every particular occasion on which they thought it could safely be done. A warning comes from the Police, and in one case from the Bench itself, and on each occasion an undertaking has been given that in street work the processions shall be continually on the move. When on the move, and where no preaching takes place, they are within the law, and will certainly receive no molestation. But in every case the undertaking has been violated, the officer removed to another town, and a fresh man sent here, with whom the police have had to begin de novo.*

On Sunday, 22 June 1884, two 'captains' – Smith and Cozens – began preaching in the Market Place to around 300 people,

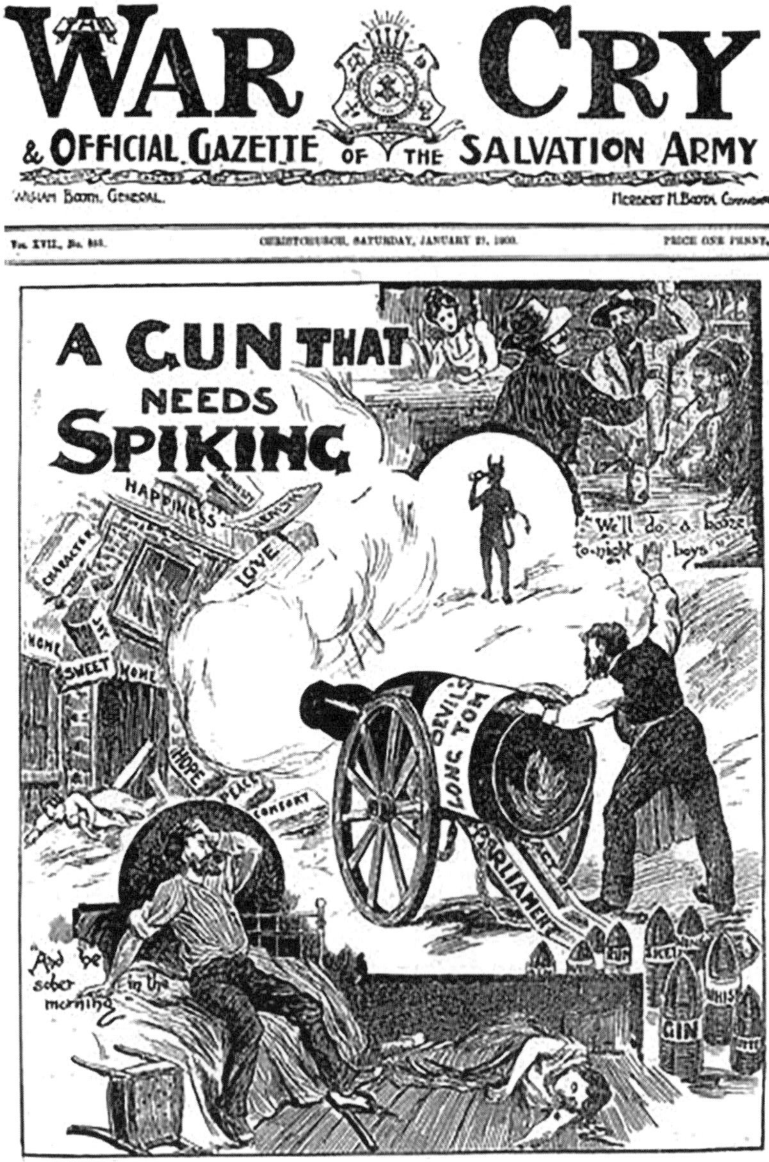

War Cry: *the official newspaper of the Salvation Army and no doubt sold on the streets of Frome.*

who stretched from the Wilts and Dorset Bank to the pillars on the pavement on the other side of the road. Constable Parsons, came by and told them they should stop and move on, or else he would take their names and addresses. Smith replied that 'we are in the Market Place, and are not obstructing the thoroughfare'. Nevertheless, within a few minutes, Smith, Cozens and the rest of the Army had 'fallen in' and marched away.

This constant violation of the law eventually reached breaking point when enough became enough and the police decided to take action and the two 'captains' were summoned under the 'Town's Police Clauses Act' to appear before Frome magistrates. The *Frome Times* reported that:

> *The law is very clear* reported *The Frome Times. The Town's Police Clauses Act provides that 'Every person who in any street, to the obstruction, annoyance, or danger of the residents or passengers, commits any of the following offences, shall be liable to a penalty not exceeding forty shillings for each offence; or, in the discretion of the Justice before whom he is convicted, may be committed to prison for not exceeding fourteen days; and any constable, or other officer appointed by virtue of this Act. Shall take into custody, without warrant, and forthwith convey before a Justice, any person who within his view commits any such offence, namely—.' Then follow a number of provisions, and the Statute proceeds thus:- 'Every person … who wilfully interrupts any public crossing, or wilfully causes any obstruction in any public footpath or other public thoroughfare.' This was the clause under which the police information was laid. It has been laid down that the word 'Street' includes any road, square, court, alley, and thoroughfare, or public passage, and means a place to which the public have a right of access. The street includes the carriage-way and footpaths at the side. The offence must be committed in the street, but the annoyance may be to 'residents', meaning occupiers of houses in the street, although they may not be in the street at the time, and it is not necessary to call such as witnesses.*
>
> *This is the law as it stands at present on this subject. Then as to street preaching. The following appears to be the rule as laid down by Judge Hawkins:- 'If held in the street, such meetings appear to stand on the same footing as other obstructions of the highway; and the general rule is, that any unauthorised obstruction, to the annoyance of the Queen's subjects (R. v. Cross), or doing any act which renders a highway less commodious to the public, is a nuisance, and indictable at common law. It is not necessary that the obstruction should be total; it is sufficient if part only, and not the whole breadth of the highway be obstructed.' In another case, it is laid down, that 'Any*

> *defence founded on a plan of constitutional right (as contended for by some of the zealous advocates of Home Missions, etc., etc.), cannot be sustained.' This is the view taken by the Leicestershire Quarter Sessions in October 1869, on a street preaching appeal – a decision which has never been challenged.*

James Smith and William Joseph Cozens appeared at the Frome petty session on Thursday 10 July 1884 charged with causing an obstruction. Bristol-based solicitor, H.R. Wansbrough was enlisted to defend them. He argued the case convincingly. It was no offence to stand and loiter in the Market Place, as charged in the summons, but the Act of Parliament was framed to meet the case of persons wilfully causing an obstruction – which his clients were not. Although one witness claimed he had seen people having to move off the pavement and go onto the road to get past the crowd, when PC Parsons was cross-examined, he had to admit that he had not seen anyone obstructed.

Taking all of this into consideration, most of the magistrates' bench – there were five magistrates present – were of the opinion that there had been an indirect obstruction, but as the Salvationists had moved on directly they were requested by PC Parsons, they would impose the smallest fine possible: sixpence. The defence counsel applied to be allowed to state a 'case' to a higher court, but this application was refused. He then asked that execution of the 'sentence' might be stayed for a fortnight or three weeks, which was granted.

Although the fine was the smallest possible, the two defendants pleaded that they did not have that amount of money. It seems more than likely that the leaders of the Frome Salvation Army branch had decided that this situation would gain a lot more publicity if the fines were not paid. The consequence of not being able to pay the fine was seven days imprisonment and the two 'captains' were duly sent to Shepton Mallet Gaol during August 1884.

> *The law is thus very clear, and even on the ground of sentiment, the Salvation Army has not a leg to stand upon. There cannot be much sympathy among right-minded people for men who wilfully evade their own solemn undertakings; but that is not the matter we are referring to. It is a question of religious freedom. In England every man has a right to worship, or not worship, in just such manner as he pleases. What he has not a right to do*

> *is to be a nuisance to his neighbours, or to any other person in the land. We should very much like the magistrates who decided the case in such an unsatisfactory way last Thursday to have to live in a house situated as near as those in the Market-place are to their nightly rows, and if they be endowed afterwards with any sentiment of love of the movement, they would certainly rank with the Jobs of any age. It is this that should rob the Salvation Army of any sentimental following in the matter. There can be none for acts that are an intolerable nuisance to the people amongst whom we live. Certainly, the able lawyer made the best of a bad case last Thursday, but it was only by importing this specious sentiment into it. In effect he said 'Look at the good intentions of my clients;' they 'are trying to do good.' There might have been the very obvious retort of the old proverb, but it is sufficient to answer that even 'good intentions' must be within the law of the land.*

Having served their week-long sentence, the two prisoners were released on Thursday 28 August 1884. They were met by a huge crowd of their fellow Salvationists, which included members from Bath, Yeovil, Bristol and Wells, as well as Frome. Two bands provided the musical accompaniment, as they made their way through the streets to the 'British Workman', where the two captains enjoyed their first post-prison breakfast.

It was no secret that the Salvation Army wanted to make as big a thing of their release as possible and several events had been organised for the men on their return to Frome. Hundreds of handbills had been printed and distributed around the town. On it was the following:

> *Coming Home, Thursday, August 28. Return of Captains Smith and Cozens from their Seven Days' Rest in Shepton Mallet gaol. Major Sowerby, 20 Blood and Fire Officers, and a Host of Red Hot Soldiers, with Brass Bands, will give them a proper welcome home. Grand Banquet at 5 p.m. Everybody come. Monster Salvation Tournament at 7.30. The boys from the gaol will wear their prison costume and relate their prison experiences. Come early.*

The two prisoners and the rest of the Salvationists arrived back in Frome around 11.30 a.m. and were then treated as the 'martyrs' they had cleverly become. During the remainder of the morning and afternoon, with only a pause for dinner, the party with the band paraded the town, drawing large crowds after them. After the 'grand banquet' the procession again formed. By now, the crowd had started to become angry, and yells and hoots greeted the procession.

Matters grew worse when the Salvationists stopped outside the police station and gave groans and hisses, while the band began playing the defiant tune of 'We Shall Conquer'. They then proceeded back to their barracks in Locks Lane, but while this had been going on, the crowd had swelled with more locals and the now enormous mob attacked the Salvationists from all sides.

Several of the Army's flags were taken and torn into a hundred pieces. The bands suffered also, with many of their instruments battered out of shape or destroyed; one of the big drums on display was cut open. When the melee was at its height, the Salvationists sent a hasty message to the police station for assistance. Only one man was at the station, and as he would have been perfectly useless in the middle of two thoroughly angry bodies, the sergeant on duty decided against sending him, much to his relief it can be imagined.

As soon as the flags had been captured and the Salvationists had escaped to their barracks, the mob gave three cheers and started a chorus of 'Rule Britannia', during which they formed in marching order and proceeded to the Market Place where they disbanded. In a very short time the town became quiet … until the next time.

CHAPTER 13

A Case of Madness

The sad and tragic tale of Captain Ryall, 1917

The most sensational scene witnessed in Frome for a number of years, probably beyond the recollection of any person now living, took place early on Sunday morning at Critchill, about a mile from the centre of the town.

The above appeared in the *Somerset Standard* dated Friday 27 April 1917, and it was indeed a sensational but tragic story that had unfolded on the previous Sunday, 22 April. The incident had occurred at Critchill House, situated on the western outskirts of Frome. This was the residence of a well-known ex-officer, Surgeon Captain William Phayre Ryall MD. As the *Standard* would later report, 'He was a man of commanding presence, a keen sportsman, and usually of genial temperament, though known to be at times of a somewhat hasty temper.'

Ryall was a barrister and soldier who had served in the Lancashire Fusiliers. At some time in his life, he had experienced an accident, which had affected his mind. The previous year he had suffered a recurring attack of this brain trouble but had recovered after medical care. On Wednesday 18 April 1917, there were strong symptoms to suggest a return of the problem, and his medical attendant, Doctor Rattray, a very well-known and popular medical man long resident in the town, was summoned to attend him.

Things seem to have settled down, but just after eight o'clock on the following Saturday night it was necessary for Dr Rattray to be called out again. Another attack had led to a violent outburst by Captain Ryall. Rattray arrived and a couple of hours later, around 11.30 p.m., Ryall was left in a calmer mood. It was deemed a serious enough incident to inform the police though and a couple of local constables paid a visit, but there seemed no reason for them to remain. As it turned out it was the calm before the storm.

A few hours later, in the early hours of the Sunday morning, the captain's wife phoned for the doctor again. On his arrival, Rattray observed how violent his patient had become and set about organising restraint. Rattray gave instructions for a magistrate to be summoned so that the necessary certificate could be issued, and for further assistance to be obtained to restrain the former military man, who was by now delirious, excitable and very aggressive.

Ryall however, perhaps overhearing and realising what was happening, flew into a violent rage and headed upstairs; the doctor's action being 'the spark to the gunpowder,' as it would later be described. He was not upstairs long before returning armed with a weapon: a short sword, the type worn by French Army bandsmen, complete with 2in, double-edged blade and heavy brass handle. He went straight to where the Dr Rattray was standing and, without warning, struck him a violent blow with the flat of the sword, aimed at his head. Fortunately, the doctor detected the movement in time to avoid the direct blow and the sword missed his head, or he would probably have been killed outright. The weapon glanced off his shoulder, badly bruising it.

'In the light of subsequent events it is necessary to state, for the information of outsiders who do not know him,' the *Somerset Standard* told readers, '*that Dr. Rattray is somewhat crippled, and therefore not physically fitted to cope with a man of Capt. Ryall's build, and the enhanced strength which his condition at the time assumed.*' The newspaper added that Rattray acted with great courage and discretion throughout this ordeal. Deciding the latter would be the better part of valour, the doctor left the house and went down the drive towards his motor to find the assistance needed to restrain the captain.

Meanwhile, the Ryall's gardener, a man named Whitmore, tried to remonstrate with his master and get him to give up the sword. The outcome was a severe blow to his arm, which badly bruised it and caused considerable swelling. No further injuries were inflicted on the gardener, however, as Ryall's attention was now directed outside towards the fleeing doctor.

Before Rattray had not gone very far down the drive, Captain Ryall had obtained another weapon, a sporting deerstalker's rifle. This was like the service rifle issued by the British Army at the time and used the same ammunition, .303 cartridges. He had also obtained a supply of high velocity, 'Mark 7' cartridges, with round-nosed, nickel-covered bullets, of the type in use by the army before the outbreak of the First World War. With a range of at least a mile, and Ryall being a capable marksman, it was a most formidable weapon.

Armed in this way, Ryall pursued the doctor down the drive, Rattray trying to limp as fast as he could to escape. When the captain got within about 20yds of his prey, he aimed and fired. Thankfully for the doctor, Ryall's state of mind affected the accuracy of his aim and the bullet merely struck the left elbow rather than any vital organs, although it still splintered the bone of the forearm, before it emerged through the wrist.

Bleeding freely, the doctor somehow managed to get back inside the house and secure himself within a room before his now highly deranged assailant could catch up. On finding himself unable to force his way in, the raging captain went back outside and fired through a window. Thankfully, there was no further injury to the doctor because, after securing the door, he had slumped half-unconscious on a couch and this position had made him harder to hit. The bullet embedded itself in the wall.

Prior to the attack on Dr Rattray, the captain's wife had made her escape and had preceded the doctor down the drive by a very short distance. It was Mrs Ryall who raised the alarm as to what was taking place back at Critchill House. Meanwhile, a cowman of the neighbourhood tried to induce the captain to see reason, but was treated with contemptuous indifference.

Ryall now had an ally. An inmate of the house, who is not of full intellect, as the *Standard* would later report, 'remained behind with the captain; and attired in night clothing, a slouch hat and motor dust coat, paraded the drive for a time.' Once the alarm had been raised by Mrs Ryall, an urgent message was sent to the police station. Police Sergeant Staple was dispatched to the house and cycled to the spot as quickly as possible. When he arrived, the captain was still in possession of the rifle, and the sergeant called out to him to put it down. Ryall told the sergeant to get away, but he refused and so presently, on a warning from bystanders watching from a safe position, the sergeant rapidly ducked in time to miss a shot, which whistled over his head. He took what cover was possible from his position in the road and two or three more shots followed without doing any harm to him.

Mr Woodland, chairman of the Frome Urban Council, arrived on the scene a few minutes after Police Sergeant Staple and, realising the gravity of the situation, returned in Dr Rattray's chauffeur-driven car to the police office to secure further aid. The doctor was still inside the locked room in the house, no doubt slipping in and out of consciousness with his arm bleeding profusely, and with no medical assistance able to reach him.

At the police station, Superintendent Gilbanks, who lived on the premises, was just dressing to come on duty when the council chairman arrived to seek his assistance and within a few minutes, he had armed himself and his orderly with pistols, a miniature rifle, and a supply of ammunition. They proceeded to the Ryalls' house, giving directions for further members of the force to follow as soon as they could be brought in.

On their arrival at Critchill House, the superintendent found that a shot aimed at the sergeant had killed a valuable horse belonging to Mr Andrew Franks, which had been grazing in the line of fire; the shot had entered the animal's head.

A large group of bystanders had by now gathered to watch events and their presence gave away the police position. The captain's attention, however, was not focused in that direction, but to another group nearby, which included colleagues of Dr Rattray, along with the summoned magistrate. He fired several bullets at the group, from his position behind a motor car, but none of them connected with their intended targets.

The superintendent realised that something needed to be done swiftly and as the captain prepared himself for another shot, the police officer made ready with the miniature rifle he had brought. As Ryall lifted his rifle to take aim once more, Superintendent Gilbanks – himself a crack shot and captain of a victorious team at a recent police match – fired at the captain's left wrist, which was extended; the bullet struck him and penetrated the wrist in the fleshy part, causing him to drop the weapon.

Although now wounded, Ryall quickly picked up his weapon again and with the cover of the police blown, began firing at them. It became clear that he was using a magazine rifle of service calibre with a capacity of ten cartridges. The wound inflicted by the superintendent on the captain, however, had all but destroyed the accuracy of his aim and so his shots went wide of where the police were taking cover; although the erratic nature of their direction meant members of the public and others who had gathered were still in danger. Thankfully, no injuries occurred.

The Royal Field Artillery marching through Frome market place to divine service, before being called for their assistance in dealing with Captain Ryall.

The superintendent, meantime, managed to fire off a second shot and scored another direct hit, as the bullet ploughed along the forearm of the captain and emerged under his arm, grazing his ribs. Ryall, perhaps realising the tables were turned on him, or else running low on ammunition, disappeared back inside the house and prepared himself for a siege.

With Captain Ryall temporarily gone from view, the superintendent ordered his men into positions that would secure the safety of the public, as well as their own. He then returned to the town to confer with Colonel the Hon. H.W. Addington, who was in command of the Artillery Depot, which had been stationed in Frome for training purposes since the previous year (they were due to pull out entirely in the next couple of weeks).

By the time Superintendent Gilbanks reached the Market Place in Frome town centre, it was 10 a.m. on the Sabbath and a large contingent of artillerymen were parading through on their way to Divine service at St John's church, situated half-way up Bath Street. A force was hastily assembled and dispatched to Critchill House to deal with the emergency. The artillerymen were in Frome to undergo twelve weeks of training, before being sent to the front lines (the First World War was by now in its fourth year). Although no doubt used to being 'fired' on during military exercises, they would now experience coming under real fire.

On arrival at Critchill the armed part of the force took up their positions, while the unarmed contingent became engaged in removing the huge number of spectators who had now gathered from the danger zones. Inside the house, the captain became aware of the artillerymen's presence and began to shoot at will; firing off what was later estimated to be somewhere between sixty and seventy rounds. The armed artillerymen, before coming under fire, had been divided into small groups and had taken up positions around the grounds to surround the house, advancing under cover to the best advantage.

The news suddenly spread around the onlookers that an artilleryman had been shot, and the removal of one of the uniformed soldiers by motor-sidecar seemed to confirm it. The truth was that the soldier had recently suffered from malaria and the excitement of the situation had adversely affected him. One artilleryman did have a narrow escape though, when a bullet fired from Ryall's rifle cut into the welt of his boot and tore off part of the sole.

These events seemed to have given confidence to Ryall and he stepped into the open to continue his onslaught, but the end was now in sight. The captain's ally, acting as scout and reporting back movements of those outside was secured and removed, and the artillerymen began to return fire. Numerous shots were fired towards the house, with two of them finding their mark. One from a rifle penetrated Ryall's thigh, and a revolver shot entered his face on one side and, traversing his jaw, came out of his neck on the other side.

As church bells around Frome sounded noon, the artillerymen moved in and, although not without some difficulty, Captain Ryall was captured, secured and removed to Victoria Hospital, located in Park Road. Here, his injuries received attention, '*and though danger is not yet at an end from possible developments in his condition,*' reported the *Somerset Standard*, '*he bids fair to recover sufficiently to appear in the court on a charge – probably of attempted murder.*'

Meanwhile, back at the house, Dr Rattray was finally able to get medical assistance for his wounds. The semi-conscious medical man was removed to his home under the care of two fellow doctors – Harris and Seddon – who had earlier hastened

The old Victoria Hospital, where Captain Ryall was taken after being 'captured'.

to the scene to render what assistance they could, and had also narrowly escaped being harmed by Ryall. Not long after, Dr Evans of Beckington arrived to see what assistance he could render, while later that afternoon Dr Swaine, a well-known specialist who had been summoned, arrived from Clifton, and performed an operation to deal with the injury.

The bone was found to have been badly splintered by the initial shot from Ryall's rifle, and it seemed unlikely that Rattray would have any use of his arm for at least a year – it was doubtful if he would ever recover its full use. Many splinters were extracted, but despite the loss of blood, the doctor showed less sign of weakness than had been anticipated. He spent one or two bad days and nights, but the newspaper could later report that his condition 'is well maintained, and that he has secured some refreshing sleep and rest, and on the whole is making satisfactory progress'.

In the aftermath, it was universally agreed that given how many bullets were fired – from both sides – that so little damage had occurred and incredibly, there had been no fatalities – at least not human.

There was also a curious coincidence surrounding the incident however, and one which was described by the *Somerset Standard.* Dr Rattray's chauffeur was a man named George Greenland and although he did not figure much in the story – beyond driving Mr Woodland, the council chairman, to the police station – his connection with the events of the day, reported the *Standard*, was remarkable. It recalled that some thirty years before he had been the victim of a similar occurrence, and suffered in almost the same way that the doctor had on this occasion. Greenland had been shot in the left elbow by a 'demented' man named Phippen, and it had been a long time before he was able to properly use it again. His assailant was tried at Bristol Assizes and found not to be responsible for his actions. He was sent to Broadmoor Criminal Lunatic Asylum, where, the newspaper understood, he was still confined.

As for the perpetrator of the most recent incident, Captain Ryall, once he was recovered enough in Victoria Hospital, he was sent to Shepton Mallet Gaol to await trial. A tragic post-script to this story is that a few months later, while still in prison, he committed suicide by jumping off a ladder.

On Thursday 27 September 1917, sometime during the afternoon, Captain Ryall was in the prison exercise yard. Nearby, were four fellow prisoners, each helping to paint the exterior frames of cell windows, and each doing so at the top of their own ladders. One of the painters came down to fetch something and while he was otherwise occupied, Ryall dashed up the ladder. The captain was so quick that neither his guard – John Adlam – or the warder in charge of the painting detail could react in time to stop him and before anyone knew, the prisoner had scrambled almost to the top of the very long ladder.

According to the inquest report, Warder Sutton – the man in charge of the painting party – then said 'Captain, you are not allowed to go up there, come down'. Although there had been an unsuccessful attempt to grab Ryall's feet as he began to climb, once he had reached a particular height, neither prison guard attempted to follow to avoid exacerbating the situation.

The prison governor came out of his office and arrived in the yard. He tried to cajole the prisoner into coming down by saying: 'Captain, come on down, you will have a visitor here in a few minutes.' It was to no avail.

Captain Ryall turned around, so that his heels were on the rungs of the ladder, and began to undress as he perched

Shepton Mallet Prison, where Captain Ryall committed suicide in 1917 by jumping off a ladder propped up against the large building in the centre. (Authors Collection)

precariously near the top. First, he took off his hat and threw it down below. Next, he took off his coat, waistcoat, his collar and his tie. He then shouted out to the large crowd gathered beneath him: 'Get out of my way, you lot of devils.' After this, he leaned forward slightly, hesitated for a moment or two, and then made a clean jump from the ladder onto the footpath below. Here, several mats had been placed to try and break his fall, should he decide to jump.

Despite landing on his feet – although whether this was on the mats the inquest record does not state – he fell over and knocked his head. He was taken to the prison hospital and a doctor was called. William Phayre Ryall, the unfortunate and no doubt mentally tortured former military man died at 7 o'clock in the evening, a most tragic end to a very tragic story.

Chapter 14

Murder on the Mount

The Killing of Mrs Thorne and Mr Bray, 1926

It was Saturday morning and Mrs Smith was feeling uneasy. She had neither seen nor heard her friend and next-door neighbour Mrs Ellen Thorne, or her two lodgers, at their normal time and as it was now 11 o'clock, she was wondering if everything was okay. As the morning wore on her uneasiness grew into worry and she confided her fears to Mrs Strickland, who lived in the house opposite. The pair noticed that there was a window open and took this as a sign that things were probably alright but eventually decided to knock on the cottage door.

'I knocked and knocked', said Mrs Strickland later,

> *but there was not the slightest stirring inside the house. I saw that the key had been put in the lock from the inside. The kitchen window is at the side of the house. I went around and peered in. At first, I saw nothing, then standing on tip toe I caught a horrible glimpse of the old man Bray lying on the floor. I was only too sure then that something dreadful had happened. Two nephews of Mrs Thorne live within a short distance of The Mount and I went to these and told them to fetch the police.*

Police Sergeant Parfitt received the information from the nephews and made his way up to the house. On arriving at Mrs Thorne's house – 8 The Mount – Parfitt climbed through the kitchen window. Once inside, he immediately found one of the lodgers, Isaac Bray, and the landlady, the owner of the house, Mrs Thorne, lying dead on the floor. There seemed to be no indications of a struggle but it looked as though terrible head injuries had been inflicted upon the couple. Supper was still laid on the table and apart from the ghastly sight of the two bodies on the floor, all was neat and tidy in the little cottage.

Sergeant Parfitt then cautiously made his way upstairs and peered into the first two bedrooms, noting that these had not been slept in. In the third bedroom however, he found the body of William Hoddinott with a severe wound to his throat; a hatchet and an open razor lay beside him. Dr Johnston and Superintendent Stewart were summoned immediately, the latter being called out of attendance at the Bath Petty Sessions. The most likely sequence of events was quickly agreed upon – William Hoddinott had killed both Mrs Thorne and Mr Bray and then taken his own life – and so it looked as though neither mystery or problem was going to present itself during the investigation – except one. Why?

Ellen Thorne was 55 years old and very well-known in Frome, described as 'genial and kindly' by those who knew her; her tragic end created profound shock among the local community. She had lived in the cottage on The Mount, for about fifteen years and was dependent for her living upon the rents paid by her two lodgers. She had a sister in Frome, the wife of a well-known tradesman, and two sons, Tom and Fred, one living in Torquay and the other in London. She was a widow – her husband Sidney, a painter, had died some time before.

The other victim, Isaac Frederick Bray, aged 70, was a member of an old Frome family and was once a reader at the Frome Printing Works. At some time in his life, he had also been landlord at the Railway Hotel in Frome. The town's railway station had opened in October 1850 and the tavern, a short distance away, had been built not long afterwards. Isaac Bray had taken over from Henry Fear in 1894 and ran the hostelry with his wife Phyllis until it was rebuilt in 1898. He had also held the licence of an establishment in Devizes.

Bray had only been lodging at The Mount a little longer than Hoddinott. He was well-known in the town of Trowbridge, where he lived for many years. He was a staunch member of the local Conservative Club and had undertaken various night watchman duties during the Great War.

William Hoddinott, aged 38, was described as 'a quiet man who did not mix with people'. It was said he had been employed as a stable-helper before the war by the Marquis of Bath at Longleat House. In 1914 he left there to enlist at the outbreak of war, and served in the Wiltshire Regiment. He saw considerable active service but survived and returned to Longleat upon demobilisation in April 1919. Sadly, like so many others, he came back a changed man.

His fellow employees told the local paper he suffered from delusions, believed he was being followed and appeared constantly afraid of something, although was never able to say what it was. On one occasion, upon entering the servants' hall, he complained that his food had been poisoned and said that he wanted it sent away to be analysed. He remained at Longleat until September 1924, when he gave three days' notice but left at once. His colleagues described him as quick-tempered, someone to be humoured and interacted with carefully and who often walked around his room all night.

Hoddinott then went into the service of a local solicitor, Martin Daniell, as a gardener, but left there in the early part of 1926. Since then, so it was reported, he had had no work and it was presumed that he lived off his savings. He had been lodging with Mrs Thorne for about twelve months. It was remarked on, by several neighbours before the murder, that he seemed to suffer from 'nerves' and was somewhat strange in his manner; he claimed himself that he had been badly affected by his war service.

Mrs Penny, wife of a local baker, who lived in Trinity Street and was the sister to Mrs Thorne, told the press that her sibling had remarked at times that her lodger was somewhat strange in his manner, although she had never expressed any fear of him. He grew more depressed and moody and although Mrs Thorne had been very patient with him, Mrs Penny said, it seems likely that Hoddinott was soon to leave the cottage as Mrs Thorne had advertised the previous week for a lodger. As he was not in receipt of unemployment benefit, it is possible that he was unable to continue paying rent and supporting himself; this lack of resources and the pressure of having to leave his home might have pushed him over the edge. He had no relatives in Frome, although there were apparently brothers and sisters living in Wales, Yeovil and Swindon.

The bodies were left in the house, which had been guarded by the police round the clock, with all the blinds drawn, since the tragedy. There was a large crowd of sensation seekers around the building when the local coroner Mr Louch arrived from Langport. He and Superintendent Stewart of the Somerset Police, who was in charge of enquiries, forced their way through

William Hoddinott who committed suicide after the crime.

Mrs. Thorne, one of the victims. (See news pages).

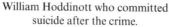

Images of the murderer and one of his victims – his landlady – appeared in the local newspapers.

the crowd, through the little gate and entered the house from the back; avoiding having to open the front door which would have exposed the horrors within to the assembled crowd.

The inquest opened on the following Monday and Mr Louch sat with a jury at Frome, so as to lead the inquiry into the terrible tragedy. Mrs Susan Strickland, a widow who lived opposite Mrs Smith and the person who had knocked on the deceased's door, was the first witness. She gave her evidence 'under the stress of emotion', explaining that Mrs Smith had come to her worried about the lack of activity by her neighbour so late in the morning. She then explained how they had looked through the window to see the table 'beautifully laid' and then to her horror, saw Mr Bray lying dead on the floor.

Sergeant Parfitt described how he had climbed through the kitchen window and found the body of Bray lying in a pool of blood on the floor, with the back of his head smashed in. He described finding the body of Mrs Thorne lying face down, also with a wound in the back of her head. In his opinion, he said, it looked as though she had been sitting at the table and had fallen from the chair to the floor. The kitchen table had been laid for three persons and the meal had been partly consumed.

Moving into the scullery, which led from the kitchen, the police sergeant found a hatchet which appeared to have been partly washed in the sink. Parfitt formed the opinion that the woman had been hit first with one fatal blow, then Bray had been struck across the table by a right-handed blow. The wound, going from left to right, must have caused his head to fall forward on to a corner of the table. He then seemed to have struggled towards the door before being struck by a terrific blow from behind. There was no sign of any argument or struggle. In response to a question from the jury foreman, Parfitt said that Hoddinott seems to have taken part in the meal and then got up suddenly to fetch the hatchet and returned to take them by surprise.

Dr Farley Dobson of Frome was called to the house at 12.30 p.m. and found the victims on the floor with large head wounds. Bray had been struck twice, the first blow glancing off his skull, while the second penetrated it; indicating great force had been used. The woman had a wound to the back of the head about four and a half inches long. Death in both cases had been instantaneous and must have happened the previous evening as rigor mortis had set in. Death in both these cases was due to skull and brain injuries.

The body of William Hoddinott was found lying behind the door of his upstairs bedroom with severe wounds to his throat; a bloodstained razor was found on a table beside him, dropped as he fell dying from what must have been an instant haemorrhage. The coroner then summed up:

> *The evidence showed that the deceased* [Hoddinott] *was a man of curious temperament. It seemed that he had been in 'gentleman's service' and did not like the idea of accepting a meaner occupation. He was getting to the end of his resources and being unable to pay the landlady had told him that he must go. No doubt this was the subject of conversation when he was seen gesticulating in the garden with Mrs Thorne. He resented the proposition.*
>
> *Mrs Thorne then goes into the house, supper is laid, Mrs Thorne sitting at one side of the table and Bray at the other. I am not able to say at which end of the table Hoddinott sat. What the conversation at the table was no one can tell. There may have been a recurrence of the discussion between Mrs Thorne and Hoddinott or Hoddinott may have wrought up into a temper. He went out, he knew where the hatchet was*

> *and returning with it he struck her from behind a violent blow to the head which left her lifeless immediately. Bray must have jumped up either with the idea of rendering some assistance or perhaps escaping, but he received a blow while at the side of the table which probably caused him to fall against it. Hoddinott then went upstairs and cut his throat. There seems to be little doubt that the wounds were inflicted on himself with great deliberation and great violence. The evidence seems to show deliberate purpose by his going out of the room to get the hatchet.*

Concluding, the coroner said that it was not for them to consider the state of Hoddinott's mind. The evidence of the delusions which led him to leave the service of the Marquis of Bath was not sufficient to justify the statement that the man's mind was permanently deranged. The coroner advised the jury to say that Hoddinott killed himself feloniously and to stop there. Regarding the cause of death of the other two, there was no doubt that only one hand could have inflicted the fatal wounds and that was the hand of Hoddinott. After a short retirement, the jury returned a verdict that Mrs Thorne and Bray died of fatal wounds inflicted by William Hoddinott and that Hoddinott killed himself feloniously.

Hoddinott was buried in the family grave in great secrecy early one Wednesday morning in September 1926, his body having been taken to the cemetery the previous night. Only two brothers and a sister were in attendance.

Thousands of people, however, witnessed the funerals of Ellen Thorne and Isaac Bray later the same day, as they lined the route between the ill-fated house and the cemetery. Mrs Thorne was laid to rest in the grave of her late husband, while Mr Bray was placed in his family's vault.

Bibliography

Barry, J., *Witchcraft & Demonology in South West England 1640–1789*, AIAA 2012

Davis, M. & Lassman, D., *The Awful Killing of Sarah Watts*, Pen & Sword True Crime 2018

Davis, M. & Pitt, V., *The Historic Inns of Frome*, Akeman Press 2015

Lassman, David, *Frome in the Great War*, Pen & Sword 2016

McGarvie, Michael, *Frome Anthology*, Frome Society for Local Study 1982

McGarvie, Michael, (ed.), *Crime and Punishment in Regency Frome*, Frome Society for Local Study 1984

Meyhew, H. & Binny, J., *The Criminal Prisons of London & Scenes of Prison Life*, Google Books 1862

Pickering, Andrew, *The Hellish Knot: Witches and Demons in Seventeenth Century Somerset*, Ape or Eden 2015

Sweet, J. W., *Somerset Tales, Shocking & Surprising*, Amberley 2011

Trench, Charles, *The Western Rising; The Account of Monmouth's Rebellion*, Prentice Hall 1969

Wigfield, W. M., *The Monmouth Rebels*, Sutton 1985

Useful Addresses

Frome Society for Local Study. Prospect House, Trudoxhill, Frome, Somerset BA11 5DP info@fsls.org.uk

Frome Museum. 1 North Parade, Frome, Somerset BA11 1AT. Tel: 01373 454 611. info@frome-heritage-museum.org

Frome Library. Justice Lane, Frome, BA11 1BE. Tel: 0300 123 2224

Somerset Record Office. Brunel Way, Norton Fitzwarren, Taunton TA2 6SF. Tel: 01823 337 600

Websites

Ancestry

Bath & District Births, Marriages and Deaths – bathbmd.org.uk

Central Criminal Court (Old Bailey) searchable database of cases – oldbaileyonline.org

Find My Past

Frome and District baptisms, marriages and burials – fromeresearch.org.uk

The Times Newspaper Archive – gale.cengage.co.uk/times.aspx

Main newspapers consulted

Bath Chronicle 1762 to date

Frome Times 1859–1886

Somerset Standard 1887 to date

Somerset & Wiltshire Journal 1855–1925

Index